DAVID ROBERTSON

DENMARK VESEY

David Robertson is the author of *Sly and Able*, a biography of former U. S. Secretary of State James F. Byrnes, and a historical novel, *Booth*. His poetry has been published in *The Sewanee Review* and other journals, and he has provided political and literary commentary to ABC News, *The Washington Post*, *Voice of America*, and A&E. He lives in South Carolina.

ALSO BY
DAVID ROBERTSON

Booth
Sly and Able

DENMARK VESEY

DENMARK VESEY

David Roberston

VINTAGE BOOKS

A Division of Random House, Inc.

New York

FIRST VINTAGE BOOKS EDITION, AUGUST 2000

Copyright © 1999 by David Robertson

The Library of Congress has cataloged the Knopf edition as follows:
Robertson, David.
Denmark Vesey / David Robertson. —1st ed.
p. cm.
Includes index.
ISBN 0-679-44288-X (alk. paper)
1. Vesey, Denmark, 1767 (ca.)–1822.
2. Charleston (S.C.)—History—Slave Insurrection, 1822.
3. Slavery—South Carolina—Charleston—Insurrection, etc.
4. Slaves—South Carolina—Charleston—Biography.
5. Afro-Americans—South Carolina—Charleston—Biography.
I. Title.
F279.C49N473 1999
975.7' 91503'092—dc21   98-31825
[B]   CIP

Vintage ISBN: 0-679-76218-3

Author photograph © Ray Barfield
Book design by Robert S. Olsson

www.vintagebooks.com

Printed in the United States of America
10   9   8   7   6   5

To Vick and Rebecca,
who gave me freedom to write

For if a slave can have a country in this world, it must be any other in preference to that in which he is born to live and labor for another. . . . Indeed I tremble for my country when I reflect that God is just: that his justice cannot sleep for ever; that considering numbers, nature and natural means only, a revolution of the wheel of fortune, an exchange of situation, is among possible events; that it may become probable by supernatural interference! The Almighty has no attribute which can take sides with us in such a contest.

—Thomas Jefferson, *Notes on the State of Virginia*, 1787

A system so oppressive could not be endured. The natural consequences followed. Deep hatred was engendered between the orders, accompanied by factions, violence, and corruption, which distracted and weakened the government. At length, an incident occurred which roused the indignation of the plebeians to the utmost pitch and which ended in an open rupture between the two orders.

—John C. Calhoun, *A Disquisition on Government*, 1853

Remember Denmark Vesey.

—Frederick Douglass, *"Men of Color to Arms!,"* 1863

CONTENTS

Contents

8 pages of illustrations will be found following page 114

DENMARK VESEY

INTRODUCTION

---◆◉◆---

The Reality of Denmark Vesey

No one thought to describe his face. For seven days during his trial and sentencing, he was kept under constant guard at the Work House, a frame building for the punishment of slaves, located near the marshes that then marked the western limit of the city of Charleston, South Carolina. No black person without a special authorization was allowed within two blocks of the building, while throughout that third week of June 1822, freemen and slaves under arrest came and gave testimony against him inside a small room on the upper story of the prison. Later that autumn, after his hanging, two of his judges published an official record of the proceedings. It totals 164 printed pages of evidence and testimony, complete with an "Introduction and Narrative." But at no point in this text did any of his judges think it necessary to describe his features. Throughout his trial and sentencing, he is officially depicted simply as a black man, and as a freeman.

The enigma of his face returned to confront the city of Charleston 154 years after his execution. In 1976, the city commissioned his portrait to be painted and placed in honor at the new municipal auditorium. The artist selected was thus presented with the problem of portraying a man of whom there was no known likeness. But this was by no means the only difficulty. "If black leaders in Charleston had searched for a thousand years," a white columnist for the *Charleston News and Courier* wrote when the art project became known, "they could not have found a local black whose portrait would have been more offensive to many white people." A letter to the same newspaper, presumably from a white correspondent, proposed that if this man deserved such an honor, "we should also hang portraits of Hitler, Attila the Hun [and] Herod the murderer of babies." Responding to this criticism, the bishop of the African Methodist Episcopal Church at Charleston replied, "We know what he intended to do to them, and we know what they did to him." The man to be pictured, the A.M.E. bishop said, was "a liberator whom God sent to set the people free from oppression." The portrait eventually was finished, and in a public ceremony it was placed in Charleston's Gaillard Auditorium. The artist solved his problem by portraying his subject facing away from the picture's frame and addressing a group of his black followers. Well over 150 years after his death, Denmark Vesey still turns his back on the twentieth-century observer.

Denmark Vesey in 1822 organized the most elaborate and well-planned slave insurrection in the history of the United States. Had it succeeded, it also would have been the most violent. Nine years before Nat Turner's slave revolt in Virginia's Tidewater district, and thirty-seven years before John Brown's raid at Harpers Ferry, Vesey planned to seize the United States arsenal and ships at harbor in Charleston, then the fifth-largest city in the nation. In preparation for this attack, he recruited perhaps nine thousand slaves in his cause. He preached to them the doctrine of negritude, the shared spiritual identity of all people of color, whether in Africa, the Americas, or the West Indies. Three months before the date of the planned uprising, he corresponded with the president of the new black Republic of Haiti, in hopes of obtaining that nation's military aid in his rebellion. On the night of the uprising, trusted house servants who were among his closest coconspirators were to assassinate the governor of South Carolina and other important state officials as they slept in their

Charleston homes. Vesey had prepared six infantry and cavalry companies of armed slaves to roam through the streets of Charleston following these deaths, and murder the entire white population, including children. The city itself was to be burned to its foundations with explosives and incendiaries he had obtained for that purpose. The sole whites to be spared would be the captains of ships seized after the revolt to carry him and his followers to Haiti or Africa.

He failed, and in the summer of 1822, Vesey and seventy-seven of his followers were hanged or imprisoned. But when the details of the Vesey plot and the fact of its near-success became known outside of Charleston, his planned actions had consequences throughout nineteenth-century American history. The then U.S. president, James Monroe, withheld diplomatic recognition of the Republic of Haiti after he learned of the plot; the United States would not grant recognition to this republic, founded on the same revolutionary principles as the United States, until 1863. A former U.S. president, Thomas Jefferson, saw in the events at Charleston a melancholy confirmation that black slavery inevitably would sunder the nation which he, in his generation, had worked to make whole; and the secretary of war in 1822, John C. Calhoun, quietly began transferring sympathetic U.S. officers and troops southward to support the slaveholding states in the coming crisis. Forty-three years later, on Good Friday, April 14, 1865, after a civil war that had claimed more than 800,000 military and civilian lives, the flag of the United States was raised for the first time since the beginning of the war over the rubble that was now Fort Sumter in Charleston Harbor. A crowd of more than four thousand people, most of them ex-slaves from the surrounding plantations, began to sing "The Star-Spangled Banner." Among them was Denmark Vesey's son.

Yet the man himself is not easily revealed. Denmark Vesey made no confession, and he spoke no final words on his gallows. Throughout his trial, as former conspirators were brought into the small upstairs room to tell what they knew, "he remained immovable," his judges wrote; "he folded his arms and seemed to pay great attention to the testimony given against him, but with his eyes fixed on the floor." After each witness finished, Vesey requested and received permission from the court to conduct his own cross-examination. In questioning each witness closely about dates of supposed conversations, he displayed what his judges characterized after his death as "great penetration and sound judgement." But Vesey never categorically denied the existence of a plot such as the witnesses described in their testimony against him; and he and his three chief coconspirators "mutually supported each other," according to his judges, with their shared byword repeated among themselves in their prison cells: "Do not open your lips! Die silent, as you shall see me do." The ferocity of Vesey's planned revolt, and his determined silence to his death, convinced one prominent historian in the mid-twentieth century that Denmark Vesey simply was insane; most probably, in the historian's view, a brain lesion developing late in his lifetime had turned "the docile slave into a revolutionary."

But he was not a slave. He was a free man, and had lived free in Charleston for twenty-two years before his planned revolt. Neither was he a young firebrand, lacking in the experience to judge the likelihood of his success in leading an insurrection. At the time of his arrest, Vesey probably was close to sixty years of age, nearly twice as old as Nat Turner. He prospered as a carpenter in the city he hoped to destroy, employing over the years several helpers; he owned a comfortable house in the same neighborhood and within three city blocks of the residence of the governor he hoped to assassinate. And, most astonishingly, he had become a free man by purchasing his own liberty from his slave-captain master with winnings he received from a ticket drawn in a Charleston lottery.

Denmark Vesey's life cannot be dismissed by regarding him as a personal or social aberration. Such apparently also was realized by his judges, who shortly after publishing their account of his trial and that of his coconspirators changed their minds and sought to recall the book. The book, *An Official Report of the Trials of Sundry Negroes, Charged with an Attempt to Raise an Insurrection in the State of South Carolina: Preceded by an Introduction and Narrative,* is now rare. One copy is at Harvard University, with a note on the flyleaf handwritten by a young Union officer, dated January 20, 1862. Captain S. M. Weld, Jr., formerly of Harvard, recorded that he had found this book in the garret of an abandoned plantation at Hilton Head, South Carolina, "two days after the battle of Port Royal." The young officer discovered it "among a number of old pamphlets and newspapers which had apparently been thrown out and forgotten by the owner. All the copies which could be found were destroyed soon after its publication—it was thought a dangerous document for slaves to see."

From the densely packed type of this early-nineteenth-century book, its pages as stiff and cracking as the sails of an old slave ship, a personality struggles to come to life, with all the singular incidents and desires of an individual. "At the head of the conspiracy stood Denmark Vesey," the book begins; "with him the idea undoubtedly originated." From its following pages, we learn that Vesey, although born either in Africa or in the Virgin Islands, was a longtime resident of the United States, and that as a teenage boy he had worked as a slave on the French sugar plantations of Haiti. He received no known formal education, but as an adult he could speak and write both English and French with eloquence, and also spoke Creole, Spanish, and other European languages. He had extensive familiarity with the Bible, and he collected pamphlets on the abolition of the slave trade. He closely read transcripts of the debates in the U.S. Congress throughout 1819–1821 on whether to admit Missouri as a slave state; he held the winning ticket in the East Bay Street lottery. In his work both as a slave and as a free carpenter, white people trusted him, and, until his arrest, some apparently liked his company. His former master, Joseph Vesey, a retired captain in the slave trade then living in Charleston, testified to the court that on first observing the young Vesey in 1781 as he was transported among a cargo of 390 slaves aboard his ship, the captain was taken with the boy's "beauty, alertness, and intelligence"; he had him brought above decks, given a change of clothes, and assigned new duties on the ship. As was customary, the new slave took his master's name. Denmark Vesey worked for Joseph Vesey in the slave trade in the West Indies and at Charleston for the next nineteen years, until buying his freedom.

We are told that by the 1820s Denmark Vesey was known among other blacks in Charleston as "the old man" or "old man Vesey." But his judges noted that during his two decades as a carpenter in the city he was "distinguished for great strength and activity," and in recruiting slaves from the outlying plantations to his conspiracy in the year before his planned revolt, this man in his late fifties sometimes traveled upward of eighty miles, probably on foot. He acknowledged seven women as his wives at foreign ports and at Charleston, and he had at least two sons and several stepchildren in the city; he was both a Presbyterian and a member of the African Methodist Episcopal Church. An early recruit to his conspiracy, later arrested and sentenced to death, lamented to his judges that "if it had not been for the cunning of that old villain Vesey, I should not be in my present situation." But another black witness testified that he once had asked Vesey whether as a free man he did not desire to emigrate to Africa. Vesey replied, according to this slave's testimony, that although a change of nation might attract other free black men, "he had not a will; he wanted to stay and see what he could do for his fellow-creatures."

We learn of Vesey only what others will tell us, and the purported facts of his life are often incongruous, sometimes narrated in fear, and always secondhand. But there is also present in all these facts the "peculiar reality," in the words of the twentieth-century historian William Freehling, in which Denmark Vesey lives both as an individual and as an historical inevitability. What if, at the beginning of the last century, winning lottery ticket number 1884 had been held by a representative of one of the great slaveholding families of Charleston—a Pinckney, a Rhett, or a Gaillard—instead of by this strangely named slave Denmark Vesey? And why, of all possible names, did his slave-trader master choose to distinguish his favorite slave by naming him after Vesey's probable place of birth, the Danish Virgin Islands? The revolt organized by this black man appears in history led not by a "Cuffee," or an "Uncle Toby," or someone with a biblically inspired name, but by a man whose first name is alien to the United States, and a reminder of the first European nation to outlaw the slave trade, two decades before the planned uprising at Charleston. And why in 1822 were individual freedom and prosperity not enough for Denmark Vesey?

With this last question, Vesey's reality continues to live into the late twentieth century. His revolt was as much an attempt to deliver a people's African identity within the United States as it was an act to deliver those people themselves from this nation's bondage. Vesey's plans could not have progressed as far as they did without the organization and membership of the African Methodist Episcopal Church, commonly called the "African Church," founded by blacks at Charleston in 1817 as a denomination distinct in forms of worship and race from the congregations of their white owners. All but one of Vesey's closest fellow conspirators were A.M.E. members, and after the city of Charleston forcibly shut down the African Church in 1818, arresting its bishop and four ministers along with 140 other members, Vesey recruited heavily from its rolls. To those recruits both within or outside of Christian orthodoxy, Vesey also preached the creed of the shared African heritage of North American black slaves. Ten of his most active recruits were African-born, and six of these went with him to the gallows. Before the night of his planned revolt, Vesey rejected the inclusion into the conspiracy of yet another African-born candidate on the grounds that "he did not associate with his countrymen." They must be as unified, Vesey told his conspirators, as the revolutionary ex-slaves of Haiti, who were nominally Roman Catholic, or the free blacks of Africa or the slaves of the West Indies, who had faith in Obeah or in Islam; for black people who desired an end to their slavery throughout the world, Vesey told them, "there was but one Minister who preached the gospel." Vesey presented himself both as that black minister and as the black messiah.

To a United States in the last decade of the twentieth century, now redefining itself as a racially and ethnically pluralistic nation, the attempted revolt of Denmark Vesey poses the starkest of public questions. To what extent is it possible to define oneself fully as an African-American? To what extent is such an identification desirable, in regard both to the self-interest of the black individual and to the majority society? To these questions, the life of Denmark Vesey gives an answer of disturbing ambiguity. In retaliation for past wrongs against his race, he was prepared to destroy a major city and all the white people within it, and to seek sanctuary only on another continent, among other people of color. *But he had not a will to go to Africa; he wanted to stay and see what he could do for his fellow creatures.* In our age, the public debate over the virtues of multiculturalism has heightened awareness of ethnic and racial heritages, and begun to correct the history of black slaves from one of passive victims to one of active resisters; but our urban centers also have become divided into explosive and mutually hostile enclaves where the innocent die with the violent. Although a majority of either white or black Americans in the twentieth century would not recognize his name, we are still remembering Denmark Vesey. His is a face that we cannot see but that is always with us.

CHAPTER ONE

———◆———

The Men from Barbados

*Negroes are the bait proper for Catching a Carolina Planter, as
certain as Beef to catch a Shark.*
— South Carolina Gazette, *9 March 1738*

A BLACK SLAVE STEPPED upon the ground that would later
be the district of Charleston. In early April 1670, the 220-ton
frigate *Carolina,* six months out from the island of Barbados,
entered the waters forming what is now Charleston Harbor. The
ship sailed up a shallow river to a point overlooked by a heavily
wooded bluff, and there about twenty white Barbadians disem-
barked as part of the first permanent English-speaking settlement in South Carolina. Although no one recorded the name,
the Barbadians had brought with them a black slave to work the
new colony.

Slavery thus was present from the beginning in South Carolina, uniquely among the North American colonies, where in all
other cases it was introduced only after their founding. And for
the next two centuries, South Carolina would maintain its preeminence. From the arrival of the white men from Barbados in
the seventeenth century to the U.S. prohibition of slave importation in 1807, over one-fourth of all African slaves brought and
sold into the United States—at least 132,918 people—entered
through Charleston or one of South Carolina's lesser ports. Hence,

among the current African-American population of the United States in the late twentieth century, roughly one in four has an ancestor who was sold as a slave at Charleston.

There is no reason to think these figures would have displeased the men from Barbados as the *Carolina* found slippage between the trees at the riverbank. They had come to South Carolina intending to grow rich on a slave economy, just as had their fathers on the small island they had left.

Barbados, a piece of "sixpence throwne down" upon a sailor's map of the eastern Caribbean, as one contemporary chronicler described it, was at the time of the Carolina settlement the most densely populated, the richest, and the most lethal of the English colonies in the New World. Established less than fifty years before the Carolina expedition, Barbados also was the first English colony to introduce the gang-labor system of black slavery into the New World. Rather than encouraging the immigration of a free peasantry, the early settlers chose to import African slaves to work the sugar fields which they were clearing on this once rain-forested Caribbean island. Barbadians, as this first generation of Englishmen called themselves, became known throughout the Caribbean as hard masters. They imposed their will upon their new African laborers by frequent floggings, brandings, and mutilations; and by thus coercing large gangs of slaves to repeat monotonously the same task for ten or eleven hours—slashing the sugarcane with curved knives, grinding the canes between heavy stones, then boiling out the dark molasses to produce crystallized white sugar—the Barbadians became rich.

By mid-century, Barbados was contributing nearly half of the refined sugar sent to the European market, and it had become the first English settlement to have formed a plantation ruling class. Within two generations, this island with a population in 1660 of forty thousand blacks and whites had produced a planter elite of about sixty-two families who controlled local politics, held the most arable land, and owned the most slaves. Practically all the European visitors to the island in the seventeenth century remarked upon the display of wealth and extravagant consumption of the Barbadian elite—behavior to be repeated, as several scholars of the South have noted, by their South Carolina descendants into the lifetime of Denmark Vesey. There was to be in common between these two ruling classes in the Caribbean and in South Carolina that same show of finery, sometimes even to the point of ostentatiousness, evident in both their choice of clothing and their lavishly furnished country estates; there was to be that same easy munificence among the ruling males in bestowing honorary militia titles upon one another, such as "Captain" or "Major." And there also was to be transported to Carolina that same unhesitating brutality, and an absolute conviction that slavery represented the most profitable economic system yet known to Western man.

The slave-generated wealth of Barbados came at an appalling cost in African lives. Throughout the seventeenth century, the island had one of the highest mortality rates for blacks in the Western Hemisphere, and, whether from disease, malnutrition, or torture, more died annually than were imported to work the great sugar plantations. Unlike their English contemporaries in Massachusetts, Barbadians seldom looked inward to their consciences, and so long as the supply of African slaves seemed illimitable, their economy appeared untroubled. What concerned the masters was the lack of arable land on which to expand their slave economy. Barbados is only 21 miles long and 14 miles wide, and with practically all of it under cultivation and concentrated within a few families, economic advancement, particularly for younger men, was limited. Accordingly, a group declaring themselves the Corporation of Barbados Adventurers wrote to England on August 12, 1663, offering to establish a colony in the unsettled lands south of Virginia, an area that had become known as "Carolina in ye West Indies."

The Barbadians promised the eight royal proprietors to expect not only "the aptness of the people here" for establishing a new plantation economy in North America but also a "number of there negroes and other servants fitt for such labor." For six years, the proprietors and the Adventurers negotiated their terms, but ultimately the Barbadian proposal financially enticed the English proprietors. A mainland colony could be supplied and populated much more cheaply from the existing plantations at Barbados than from Europe; accordingly, the proprietors ceded to the Corporation of Barbados Adventurers the exclusive right to settle Carolina with grants of 150 acres to each Adventurer, with an additional 150 acres granted him for each servant transported. The philosopher John Locke, secretary to one of the proprietors, devised an elaborate constitution for the new colonists, a copy of which the Barbadian Adventurers carried with them. Among other stipulations, it promised religious freedom to all residents of the colony, whether black or white. In late 1669, three ships carrying colonists sailed from Barbados, of which only one, the *Carolina,* bearing its black slave with an unrecorded name, succeeded in reaching the new colony on the South Atlantic coast.

The grant of 150 acres to the master of each servant transported to Carolina was the device by which the Barbadians turned their tiny encampment into a slave colony. Early on, the Corporation of Barbados Adventurers had obtained a written concession from the royal proprietors by which it was made explicit that in granting 150 acres for every "able man servant" transported to Carolina, the proprietors affirmed "we mean negroes as well as Christians." Within a year of the first settlement, more than a hundred other colonists arrived from Barbados, bringing their black slaves with them. John Locke, reporting back in England to the royal proprietors of news he had received from Carolina, noted the arrival in June 1671 of the colony's new governor from Barbados. "Sir Jo Yeamans intends to stay all the winter," Locke wrote. "He has brought negroes and expects more."

The white masters marked out the boundaries of what they anticipated would become a world port upon a narrow and sandy peninsula extending into the ocean bay, and, in honor of the English monarch Charles II, named their settlement Charles Town. (The spelling was changed to Charleston after the American Revolution.) Carolina attracted white immigrants from the other English islands in the Caribbean, from England, and from Ireland, but the early Barbadians dominated both public offices and private wealth. Their importation of African slaves matched, then eventually surpassed, the number of free immigrants, and landholdings among the Barbadian families increased proportionately.

Nor did the Carolina plantation owners from Barbados limit themselves to enslaving only Africans. The bondage of Native Americans was practiced throughout North America, but Carolina within a few years of its settlement gained the distinction of enslaving more Indians than any other of the Thirteen Colonies. By the early eighteenth century, the Barbadians had established a lively trade in Native American slavery, having captured and sent thousands in shackles down to Charles Town for export to the Caribbean islands for use as hunting or fishing guides, and importing black laborers from these same islands to be used as agricultural slaves in Carolina. These practices, along with the Carolina colonists' immediate attempts to circumvent the religious freedoms proposed in the colonial constitution, alarmed the royal proprietors and their philosopher secretary. "The Barbadians," remarked John Locke in England, "endeavor to rule all."

The small community that the Barbadians ruled continued to grow in slave and free population until by the mid-1700s it was the fourth-largest city of the colonies. Charles Town, which by 1740 was the capital of a colony with at least thirty thousand black slave inhabitants, succeeded even beyond the ambitions of the planters from Barbados. The city exported indigo, rice, and, later, cotton on a world scale, and the peninsula began to be crowded with two- and three-story houses erected in the distinctive Charlestonian architecture of walled gardens, piazzas, and elaborately designed private doorways concealed from the street. Many were town houses built by owners of plantations farther in the Carolina interior, who escaped the tropical heat or the tedium of rural winters by retreating for holidays to Charles Town. The influence of these English-speaking settlers from Barbados was succeeded by a wave of French Huguenots, and these Protestant immigrants became numerous enough to support three French-language newspapers and a French theater. And, in delayed fulfillment of John Locke's insistence that the Barbadian founders practice religious tolerance, Charles Town became a sanctuary from the late 1600s for Sephardim and other Jewish refugees from Europe. The city eventually contained the largest community of Jews of any urban settlement in colonial North America. Charles Town was still smaller in population than Boston, Philadelphia, or New York, but by the eighteenth century this thriving southern port was arguably the most cosmopolitan trading center of North America.

Charles Town was also cosmopolitan in its slavery. When each of the groups of white immigrants arrived in the city, they either brought with them or imported their African slaves. The new slave arrivals from the Guinea coast spoke the languages of present-day Angola, Togo, Benin, and Nigeria. Some were Muslims and left evidence that they also spoke and wrote Arabic. The blacks shipped from the Caribbean into Carolina by their Barbadian or French masters talked among themselves in a form of Creole and were known by both the blacks and whites at Charles Town as "the French negroes." And distinct among all other languages heard among blacks at the city's wharves and on her crowded streets was Gullah, an emerging amalgam of English and African words having an African-based syntax, used exclusively by slaves on the plantations of the Carolina and Georgia Sea Islands. A century later, Denmark Vesey used his mastery of the French and Gullah languages to spread the news of the coming slave revolt among the inhabitants of the Carolina low country.

To the Charlestonians of European descent, their city, with its complex population and growing wealth, was a new metropolis of the eighteenth century, in succession to the international ports of Amsterdam and London. In both its exercise of law and its physical appearance, however, the city could not deny its Caribbean origins. Legal power was encoded in Charles Town's comprehensive slave law, enacted within the first generation of the colony's founding and copied almost word for word from an earlier Barbadian statute. This slave law, which established the legal precedent for Denmark Vesey's subsequent prosecution and execution a century later, authorized the use of whipping, branding, or the splitting of noses for black slaves who offered violence against their white masters; for those who attempted the most feared of crimes, insurrection against the Carolina white ruling class, a trial under punishment of death was to be conducted not within the usual court system of jury men but by a special tribunal of "freeholders."

The streets of Charles Town as well as its laws made immediately apparent to any new visitor that this slave city was not a typically developing North American port. Unlike the brick walkways of New York City or the ballast-stone pavements of Philadelphia or Boston, the principal streets of Charles Town were covered (as they would continue to be into the early twentieth century) with a mixture of sand and finely crushed seashells. It was an inheritance from the city's Caribbean founding, and practically all northern visitors for the next two hundred years remarked on this unique white covering spreading over the urban peninsula; as an obdurate and crystalline reality it permeated even into the interiors of one's pockets and the folds of one's bed-clothes, and in the noonday sun the white sand made the streets dazzling and difficult to countenance. But it was a reminder also of the whiteness of Charles Town's growing wealth, stacked in high rows for export at the city's wharves in 500-pound bales of white cotton and 525-pound barrels of white rice, cultivated by black slaves and loaded by them onto ships; and it was a reminder of the whiteness of the city's economic elite, of the hard merchants and planters from Barbados who had sailed here from the Caribbean and accumulated their fortunes in Carolina.

THE BARBADIAN FOUNDERS of Charles Town left a third inheritance for Denmark Vesey's later revolt: a black majority. The original land grants were a strong inducement to import as many black slaves as possible into Carolina, and the economic success of the gang-labor plantation system meant easy credit to subsequent white arrivals willing to pledge future crops in exchange for immediate ownership of slaves. Possibly as early as the second generation from the Barbadians' arrival, blacks were a majority in the Carolina colony. The number of slave imports from the Caribbean proved inadequate, and the original Indian slaves died or were sold off. As a consequence, Charlestonians began to prefer "saltwater blacks" and importing firms were established at Charles Town to ship blacks directly to the city from the African western coast. White immigrants early in the eighteenth century noticed the increasingly slim minority that exercised control over the colony's majority inhabitants. "Carolina," noted a Swiss immigrant upon his arrival at Charles Town in 1737, "looks more like a negro country than like a country settled by white people."

White planters and merchants at Charles Town thus were effectively caught in an economic trap, tightening one hundred years later, during the lifetime of Denmark Vesey. Having speculated their land and crops in exchange for slaves, the whites were obliged each generation to import even more bondsmen to clear additional land and to produce rice and cotton ever more cheaply. But having created a slave majority, the white owners had made their own position physically and demographically perilous. Psychologically, white Charlestonians reacted to their situation by expressing revulsion for the blacks with whom they shared their narrow peninsula. Privately, they expressed their fears of a possible slave insurrection.

"Is it possible that any of my slaves could go to Heaven, and must I see them there?" The Reverend Francis Le Jau recorded this startling question by one of his female parishioners shortly after his arrival in Charles Town in 1706. Le Jau had come to Carolina as a young rector sent by the Church of England in his private hopes, as he wrote in his journal, of "instructing the poor and ignorant from among the white, black and Indians." As he settled in residence among the wealthy plantation owners who were his sponsors, however, Le Jau recorded his despair at converting his white parishioners from their received beliefs. "I cannot to this day," he wrote in his diary, "prevail upon some to make a difference between Slaves and free Indians, and Beasts." Later in the century, the Boston lawyer Josiah Quincy recorded his experience as a dinner guest at the Charles Town mansion of Miles Brewton. Brewton had been among the first of the city's residents to establish a firm importing African slaves, and at the time of his dinner party he possessed one of the largest fortunes in North America. Upon entering the Brewton mansion with the other guests, Quincy encountered "the grandest hall I ever beheld," and he found the wines served during the meal "the richest I ever tasted." But what particularly interested him was the conversation of his fellow guests at the table; many white Charlestonians, he wrote, expressed "great fear of an insurrection." Throughout the eighteenth century, Charlestonians of Brewton's economic class considered a project of cutting a canal across the neck of the harbor's peninsula, thereby making their city an island; such a canal would give Charles Town "the appeal of Venice," and, its promoters reasoned, also provide a barrier "against a negro insurrection."

This engineering feat proved beyond the abilities of the Carolina government, but, with two notable exceptions, Charles Town throughout the 1700s remained free from the threat of a black insurrection. What was needed for revolt, and what Denmark Vesey later provided, was, first, a messianic leader who could combine Christianity, Islam, and elements of African religion into a moral crusade for freedom, and second, the organizational skills to arm the blacks and to deploy against Charles Town the force of their numerical superiority. As the decade of Vesey's arrival in the city approached, both conditions began to take form.

The religious leaders for black freedom appeared, surprisingly, among white planters. The Barbadian founders were strong Church of England believers, but despite their dominance, a few Dissenters and evangelicals had taken advantage of John Locke's promise of religious tolerance to travel to Carolina. Among them was George Whitefield, a young Anglican evangelist from England who was described by contemporary accounts as preaching with extraordinary "Flame and Power." Whitefield arrived at Charles Town in the spring of 1740, and immediately he began preaching to large crowds in the city to give up their patronage of "jewelers and dancing masters." Nor did he limit his criticisms only to Charles Town residents' well-known fondness for opulence. Considering himself a "*crying Voice*, to bid the World repent," Whitefield later that same year published an open letter addressed to the inhabitants, among other southern colonies, of "North and South-Carolina." In his letter, Whitefield castigated slave owners for their "abuse and cruelty to the poor negroes." Citing examples of plantation owners who were "monsters of barbarity," Whitefield cautioned the Carolinians that they were fortunate that the slaves had "not more frequently risen up in arms against their owners." He wrote that he heartily prayed to his God that the blood of white people not be so spilt; but should blacks rise up and take the lives of their owners, he wrote, "all good men must acknowledge the judgement would be just."

Whitefield subsequently returned to England, but he left behind a strange convert in Hugh Bryan, a wealthy forty-one-year-old rice planter who lived sixty miles from Charles Town. Bryan had supported Whitefield in the evangelical work in Carolina that became known in the other colonies as the Great Awakening, and after the evangelist's departure, Bryan's thoughts at his South Carolina plantation turned increasingly to religion. A recurrent quotation in his journals became a passage from Job: "Who can bring a clean thing out of an unclean?" Undeniably, a sense of personal sin was becoming linked in Bryan's mind with the historical transgression of black slavery. He later wrote in his journal:

> Bathe my soul in the fountain of His blood, and take away all my guilt; so I shall rejoice in Thee for ever. Was enabled, by the divine assistance, to speak tonight with freedom to my poor negroes, and to pray with them, with some enlargement of heart.

Neighbors near Bryan's plantation began complaining in late 1741 to the Charles Town authorities of the "great Assemblies of Negroes" whom he was heard leading in shouts, singings, and exhortations. A group of travelers passing by Bryan's plantation in December 1741 reported hearing "a Moorish slave woman . . . singing a spiritual near the water's edge." Bryan himself was reputed to be filling the minds of his plantation blacks with "a Parcel of Cant-Phrases, Trances, Dreams, and Revelations." At some time probably in the late fall or early winter of 1741, Bryan retreated into the woods, announcing his intention to live there several days, "barefooted and alone with his pen and ink to write down his prophecies."

Bryan returned from the woods bearing "a whole Volume of his Prophecies," which he claimed to have received there from "many Days' intimate Converse with an invisible Spirit." He promptly sent this only copy of his revelation to colonial officials at Charles Town. It could not have been comforting reading. In his book, Bryan prophesied the coming "Destruction of Charles Town and Deliverance of the Negroes from their Servitude." Eighty years before the attempted revolt of Denmark Vesey, he claimed to have had a vision of Charles Town destroyed by "fire and sword." News of his prophecies spread privately like a secret fire among other Carolina whites and blacks, and there were rumors Bryan had spent his days in the woods collecting and distributing weapons for use by his "African hosts" in the coming revolt. Bryan himself insisted only that his message was the same as it had been since the autumn of 1741: "The cry is Repent, turn you, now is the accepted time."

Reaction from Charles Town was swift. Sheriffs were dispatched to arrest Bryan and the few other planters attracted to his revivalism. Miles Brewton, the wealthy Charles Town merchant who entertained so lavishly, was directed to buy and store gunpowder at guarded sites around the city for its defense. The book of prophecies itself apparently was destroyed by the colonial government as an act of public safety.

Bryan subsequently recanted, in early 1742, in an open letter addressed to Brewton and other public officials, confessing his earlier preaching to have been a "Delusion of Satan." No reason other than satanic influence was given for his actions, and Bryan therefore begged as a repentant sinner that "your Honors will the more easily pardon me in this Thing." Whether his conversion came from fear of imprisonment or fear for his soul, his display of deep contrition was probably what led the colonial authorities to spare him. The authorities also were amused by the report that Bryan, in imitation of Moses, had waded into the Atlantic surf with a walking staff, commanding the waters to part for his black and white followers to walk with him toward freedom. He had nearly drowned. He was allowed to return to his plantation, and his slave ownership, and for the remainder of a lengthy life in South Carolina, nothing more was heard from him as a religious prophet.

But the documentable fervor among the participating slaves in the religious revivals of the 1740s, and as well the undeniable alarm felt by Charles Town officials, demonstrate that both races anticipated a time close at hand when a messianic figure—probably by necessity a black man—would rise up to lead the slaves into revolt.

Charles Town authorities had reacted in 1741 to Bryan's brief conversion with such alarm because less than two years earlier South Carolina had experienced its most serious slave insurrection to date. Gathering by prearranged plan, a group of about twenty slaves had met by the banks of the Stono River, within twenty miles of Charles Town, early on Sunday morning, September 9, 1739. Under the leadership of an Angolan slave known only by the English name of Jemmy, the group broke into a country store, seized arms and gunpowder, and beheaded the white owners. Raising the shout of "Liberty!" and displaying a large banner, the original group recruited other slaves from neighboring plantations and announced their intention to fight their way to Spanish Florida, where they would be received as free men. Now numbering perhaps about one hundred, the group set out on the main road south to St. Augustine. Some plantation owners in their path were hidden by their sympathetic slaves; some whites were captured but spared because of their earlier kindly treatment of blacks; and some masters were shot or hacked to pieces on the spot.

By sheerest coincidence, the armed slaves happened to meet

the same Sunday the lieutenant governor of colonial South Carolina, traveling on horseback on the same road on his way to open the legislative session at Charles Town. After a narrow escape, this official succeeded in raising an alarm among white plantation owners, many of whom were attending Sunday-morning Anglican church services. A group of from twenty to one hundred planters was mustered, and the rebellious slaves were confronted at a river crossing. In an exchange of gunfire, whites killed or wounded at least fourteen blacks, but a large body of slaves crossed the river and continued southward. Many of the blacks who did not succeed in crossing the river were captured, interrogated, and given an "easy death." In the following days, the Charles Town militia arrived and, according to local reports, "kill'd twenty odd more, and took about 40." By the end of the month, the Stono Rebellion was officially declared at a close, and there is no evidence that any of the rebels ever succeeded in reaching Florida and their freedom. The slave leader Jemmy apparently was executed, along with most of his followers.

Despite its success in crushing the Stono River Rebellion, the colonial government knew it had reasons to worry. For the first time, a charismatic slave leader had arisen to organize blacks in South Carolina along national or religious lines for a violent revolt against slavery. In a period of a week, these rebels had fought two pitched battles against their armed masters and the local militia, inflicting almost as many casualties on whites as they themselves suffered. And, despite the public assurances that autumn by the Charles Town government that the Stono River Rebellion was at an end, a few surviving members of the rebel band were still at large and unapprehended until months after Christmas 1739.

The Stono River Rebellion had demonstrated at least the possibility of organizing a widespread slave revolt, but to later South Carolina blacks such as Denmark Vesey, it was also a generational memory to expect no mercy from their white masters should a revolt fail. The old Barbadian slave code, adopted in South Carolina in 1696 and revised several times since, was applied with particular severity to the rebels the white planters succeeded in catching. According to one account, the planters, celebrating their victory and drinking heavily along the twenty-five-mile road back to Charles Town, took their black prisoners and "cutt off their heads and set them up at every Mile Post they came to."

SOUTH CAROLINA APPEARED to be free from any other major organized slave revolts throughout the 1700s. The American Revolution temporarily interrupted the African slave trade, but the city known as Charleston after the war emerged with its fortunes and its trading connection intact. The last decades of the eighteenth century were the beginnings of the economic golden age of Charleston, the city becoming perhaps the third most populous and certainly the richest urban settlement in the United States. Charleston resumed its role as the preeminent North American port for the purchase of slaves, and in the enjoyment of its slave-generated wealth, the city deserved its description by evangelist George Whitefield as a heaven for "jewelers and dancing masters" and hell for sober-minded men.

"This small society of rice and cotton planters at Charleston," Henry Adams later wrote of the city, "with their cultivated tastes and hospitable habits, delighted in whatever reminded them of European civilization." With the close of the war, British luxury items were once more welcomed in Charleston, and, Adams added, English visitors to the city "long thought it the most agreeable in America." Charleston underwent a post–revolutionary war building boom, with mansions rising at the farthest tip of its civic peninsula in an exclusive residential district then known as White Point, which twentieth-century tourists would know as the Battery and as the heart of the city's historical district. Taverns and other public houses of this period regularly advertised wide selections of syllabubs and Madeira wines, and, in imitation of London's famous recreational park, Charleston even boasted an identically named Vauxhall Gardens for the exhibition of fireworks, concerts of eighteenth-century music, and the display of animal oddities.

Despite this luxury, the jaws of an economic trap, having traveled from the Caribbean, were tightening upon this port city: African slaves continued to be purchased on credit in order that even more slaves could be bought. But, given the protection of slavery by the newly ratified U.S. Constitution, the rising world market for cotton and rice, and the expansion of gang-labor plantations into the southern frontier, white Charlestonians either chose to ignore the consequences of their trap or were oblivious to it. Incidents such as the Stono Rebellion and the straying of souls such as Hugh Bryan were considered unfortunate aberrations. Slave ships with their human cargoes continued to dock monthly in Charleston's harbor, and their arrivals and points of origin were reported regularly in the *Charleston Courier* and *South Carolina Gazette*. Most of these slaves were sold at curbside auctions, along such major thoroughfares as Meeting Street, Exchange Street, or Queen Street, all within sight of the rising steeple of St. Philip's Anglican Church, the original house of worship of the city's Barbadian founders.

On the afternoon of September 24, 1783, the *South Carolina Gazette* reported the safe arrival at Charleston of two ships, the *Polly* and the *Eagle*, bearing a cargo of 104 slaves from the African coast and the Caribbean. The cargo of slaves was scheduled to be sold within a week "at Mrs. Dewee's, No. 43, Queen-street." The importation and sale of these blacks was being handled by a recently established merchant, Captain Joseph Vesey.

CHAPTER TWO

———— ◆ ————

A Place Called Charleston in the Christian Language

Poor men went in ships and became rich, it didn't matter how. . . .
—William Faulkner, on slave captains,
Absalom, Absalom!, *1937*

WITH THE DOCUMENTED appearance in 1783 of Captain Joseph Vesey at Charleston, the historically buried life of his slave Denmark Vesey also begins in part to emerge. Vesey's white master, a former slave captain, had retired from the sea by 1783 and purchased a residential lot in Charleston to pursue a second career as a maritime merchant and an occasional retailer in black slaves. Thereafter, the early life of Denmark Vesey, who was approximately sixteen years old at the time and who had been the captain's property since 1781, can be discerned at least in silhouette against the populous city. Charleston was demographically and literally an African-American community during Denmark Vesey's early adulthood; and his growing recognition of black numerical strength and cultural identity within this city eventually would bring him forth as an historically distinct individual and as an aspiring liberator of his people.

But between his arrival in 1783 as another man's property and his purchase of freedom in 1800, Denmark Vesey would live seventeen years a slave in Charleston. These years of his life, as is true for many other blacks, therefore remained buried—seldom documented, or described only in the voices, often hostile, of one white master talking to another. One wonders, for example, about the true name and unrecorded biography of the slave known as Jemmy, who organized the Stono Rebellion, or about the "Moorish slave woman" whom white travelers reported hearing singing strange hymns to other black slaves at Hugh Bryan's plantation; but historically, these individuals can be perceived only in terms of their interactions with whites, and in how their white masters chose to record their actions.

Similarly, the early life of Denmark Vesey can be retrieved only in terms of the history of the city in which he lived as a slave, and in the records of the particular white man who owned him for seventeen years. What sort of master was Captain Joseph Vesey? Was he relatively humane, or a sadist? And for Denmark Vesey, what were the possibilities of becoming a free black man in Charleston?

Captain Joseph Vesey was described in 1781, when he was about thirty-four years old, as a noticeably light-complexioned man of above average height. He was born in Bermuda, and this island, located north of the Caribbean West Indies, never supported the large sugar plantations or black slave populations of the tropics; instead, white men made their livings by shipbuilding and by supplying the West Indies and North America with agricultural staples and with slaves. Joseph Vesey also followed the sea, sailing as master or captain of slave ships for at least thirteen years before buying a residence in 1783 in Charleston. His ports of call during these years included the slave markets at Barbados, South Carolina, Haiti, and possibly West Africa.

Captain Vesey was apparently a sociable man, and was trusted and liked at least by other whites. (A contemporary relative had at this time become the first rector of Trinity Church in New

York City, and the present-day Vesey Street in lower Manhattan is named after this relative of the Charlestonian slave captain.) Joseph Vesey, despite financial reversals, was able to obtain credit at Charleston, both when he was at sea and when he became a permanent resident; and in an age when women almost always survived their spouses, Vesey married and outlived four wives. He appears to have been an honest man at his business of slave-trading. In fact, the captain's honesty in a slave sale in 1781, two years before he settled in Charleston, resulted in his obtaining an individual human property, and thus Joseph Vesey's name becoming historically linked to the future insurrectionist, Denmark Vesey.

Captain Vesey had sailed that year to the port of Cape Français on French St. Domingue, later the Republic of Haiti, with a cargo of 390 slaves. Among them was a black boy approximately fourteen who said his name was Telemaque, or so the sound of his name registered to the ears of his masters. Telemaque and the other blacks originally had been purchased at the Danish Virgin Islands, with the intention of selling them to the French owners of the sugar plantations at St. Domingue. Telemaque's fate was to be different, however. Four decades later, when Telemaque had become Denmark Vesey, testimony at his trial recalled how Captain Vesey and the other officers had noticed the beauty and intelligence of the fourteen-year-old slave, and how the captain had approved bringing the boy above decks, allowing him into the officers' cabin, and providing him with finer clothes.

The motivations of this act were not recorded at the trial. Cruel men often make the best sentimentalists, and the preferential treatment Telemaque received may be just an instance of eighteenth-century sentimentality. However he was used, it appears that during the short passage from the Danish islands to St. Domingue, the captain and his crew treated Telemaque as something like an indulged pet.

Testimony at the trial in Charleston in 1822 recalled that when the ship docked at Cape Français, "Captain Vesey, having no use for the boy, sold him among his other slaves." Telemaque was sent away to chop sugarcane, twelve hours a day under a tropical sun, presumptively for the rest of his life. Captain Vesey returned to the Virgin Islands to pick up another load of slaves.

About three months later, however, when the captain again returned to Cape Français in 1781, he was confronted by an angry plantation owner. Telemaque had proved totally unsuitable for work in the sugar fields, and had suffered epileptic fits. A French physician confirmed the diagnosis, although never again in his life would Denmark Vesey display the slightest symptoms of epilepsy. Captain Vesey apparently accepted the judgment without protest, refunded the plantation owner his payment for an unsound slave, and took repossession of Telemaque. He renamed the boy Denmark Vesey, appointed him as his personal assistant aboard the slave ship for two years, and regarded him as a valuable slave at Charleston for seventeen more years.

From these barely extant legal summaries or preserved ship manifests two centuries old, Denmark Vesey begins to emerge as a distinct individual from the anonymity of slavery or the agricultural graveyard of the sugar fields. The incident at Cape Français tells us as much about him on his own terms as in the terms of his masters. For instance, at his trial in 1822, his judges would note of Denmark Vesey that "among his color, he was always looked up to with respect and awe"; but apparently even as an adolescent he provoked a similar response among whites. Second, one can infer perhaps a grudging respect or at least a salt's grain of affection on the part of Joseph Vesey toward his returned slave. The captain surely must have realized within a few months that Denmark Vesey's supposed epilepsy in the sugar fields had been a charade; but there is no evidence that he ever tried to resell the young man, with a caution to a buyer that this slave had a history of malingering. Nor is there evidence that Captain Vesey punished his young slave for his deception and inconvenience to his master.

Most important, Denmark Vesey was installed above decks as a black person of some authority and protection aboard a slave ship. This position, and his known facility with languages, give an indication of where he was traveling in 1781–82, before his master settled with him in Charleston. A fellow black later told the Charleston court that Denmark Vesey "had, I am told, in the course of his life, seven wives and had traveled through almost every part of the world with his former master, Captain Vesey, and spoke French with fluency." Considering his position and language skills, and his master's financial needs, it is probable that in these two years aboard a slave ship Denmark Vesey made his first voyage to Africa.

The moneymaking opportunities in importing black human beings were shifting directly to Africa's west coast, and Captain Vesey would have noticed this market change by the time he had reacquired his slave. Judging by his earlier ports of call, the captain had made his living by transporting cargoes of blacks from one sugar island to another. These slaves either had been born on the Caribbean islands, as was probably Denmark Vesey, or had been "seasoned"—physically recovered from the horrors of the Middle Passage across the Atlantic—by a few weeks' residence on the islands. But by the closing decades of the eighteenth century, Charleston emerged as the major slave market in North America. Charlestonians preferred "saltwater blacks," imported directly from Africa, and distrusted slaves imported from Barbados, the Virgin Islands, or Jamaica, all of whom had histories of rebellion. The city established its own "seasoning" camp for blacks on a small island near Charleston Harbor. Perhaps as a consequence, Captain Vesey's calls at ports in the West Indies after 1781 became much less frequent, or else they have simply not been recorded; and although presumably he continued at sea as a slaver, nothing was heard of him for months at a time, until he appeared at Charleston in 1783 with two shiploads of blacks from the African coast, and a lesser number from the Caribbean.

Denmark Vesey's facility with languages would have made him a valuable, almost indispensable, addition to the crew of an Africa-bound slave ship. The young Vesey certainly must have had some knowledge of Danish, French, and English as a matter of survival; and as a mature man, he was known to be deeply literate in English and French and possibly also conversant in Gullah and Creole. Slave ships usually carried such a multilingual crew member or elevated bondsman on their outward voyage to translate as they did their business on the African coast. Slave captains such as Joseph Vesey seldom ventured into the African interior to collect slaves themselves; instead, human cargoes were bought at fortified pens along the African coast. At these holding areas, called "factories," the language of commerce could be French, Portuguese, Arabic, or a creolized African of slave-trading black despots. To have at his side a young black of notable handsomeness who also had a facility for new languages would have been a comfort to Joseph Vesey as he conducted business at these savage international ports.

What was witnessed by the young Denmark Vesey, if he did make a trip to Africa as interpreter during the years 1781–1783, has not been recorded. The slave trade succeeded in Africa largely because some black traders chose to cooperate with white ship captains; perhaps Vesey's doctrine of negritude came from the observation that blacks united could have curtailed the trade. Or perhaps Vesey's later insistence upon the genocide of all whites at Charleston was a result of the atrocities by whites he had witnessed. The brutality and degradation of the international slave trade is well attested by other contemporary sources. Sailors on other eighteenth-century commercial vessels swore that on a calm sea they could smell a slave ship five miles away, before it became visible; and for reasons of either hygiene or superstition, many white seamen refused to ship out on a vessel that had previously been used as a slaver. Nor was the life of a black human being of any more consequence to white masters upon the open sea than it was in the sugar fields. Several years before Joseph Vesey made port at Charleston, another slave captain, concerned that his black cargo would not survive the "seasoning," simply dumped his unwanted slaves overboard. The Charleston newspapers later complained of the black corpses littering the area's beaches and marshes.

No such misadventures befell the *Polly* or the *Eagle* in 1783, apparently, and the two slave ships under the charge of Joseph Vesey delivered their cargoes of African and Caribbean slaves for sale at the Widow Dewee's house. The captain subsequently advertised a slave ship for sale, purchased an undeveloped lot of land in Charleston, and retired from the sea. Slavery had not made Joseph Vesey a rich man, but he was moderately prosperous and respectable. He was appointed to several responsible civic positions by the Charleston city government, and he was listed in the 1790 census as head of a household of four free persons of color and eight slaves, presumably including the young Denmark Vesey. Captain Vesey married his third wife, and descendants eventually would spread across the United States, particularly the Midwest. He became a communicant of Christ Episcopal Church, located just outside of Charleston, and was buried there in 1835, having outlived his executed slave by thirteen years.

Fate was more abrupt for Denmark Vesey. Charleston was, by the necessity of slavery, now his permanent residence; realistically, by age sixteen he could never have expected to see again his mother or father in the West Indies, if in fact he had ever known his parents, or if they had not been sold into the cargo of another slave ship. Even his original name, which his white masters had rendered as Telemaque, no longer existed. Hereafter, he would be known in Charleston only as Denmark Vesey, identifiable as the property of the white Vesey household.

For the next seventeen years, Denmark Vesey worked as a slave in this "place called Charleston in the Christian language," as a South Carolina Muslim slave and possible acquaintance of Vesey later described the city. Vesey learned the valued skills of a carpenter, helping to construct the ships or buildings at this expanding slave port. Remarkably, because it was illegal for a slave to do so, he also learned to read and write with great discernment. And after his release from bondage Denmark Vesey secretly began his plans to destroy Charleston.

Denmark Vesey's new city of residence was the most thoroughly Africanized urban center in the United States, and it was governed as a miniature police state. The black majority that had made South Carolina sui generis among the thirteen colonies continued as the new republic unabatedly imported slaves through Charleston. In the first U.S. census in 1790, the Charleston District reported a population of 15,402 whites and 51,585 black slaves. By 1800, the numbers were 18,768 whites and 63,615 blacks. In the late eighteenth and early nineteenth centuries, many of these new slaves remained within the greater Charleston district to supplement or replace the black labor pool among the rice and cotton plantations surrounding the peninsular city. As early as 1780, for instance, the city of Charleston contained more black people than the black populations of Philadelphia, Boston, and New York City combined.

The 8 to 9 percent of the white population that controlled Charleston's wealth and political power created a police apparatus that would have made their Barbadian ancestors proud. As a slave, Denmark Vesey would have been forbidden to appear in daylight on the city streets wearing fine clothes, smoking a cigar, playing a musical instrument, or carrying a walking stick. Each evening at about dusk, a young black was sent outside the city's Guard House, or police station, to beat out a loud tattoo on a drum. This was the signal to all blacks within Charleston's city limits to disappear from the public streets until after sunrise the next day. Any black caught violating this night curfew without a written pass from his owner would be sent to the Work House, where he would be whipped and jailed until the master paid a small fine the following day. Of course, all southern antebellum cities employed both a day and a night watch to control slaves, but the local ordinances seem to have been enforced at Charleston with particular zeal. A frequent complaint of white Episcopalians and Presbyterians within the city was that after leaving their carriages and black coachmen at the curb on Sunday mornings, they would return after services to find their slaves missing, having been arrested by the guard for loitering and sent to the Work House.

The Work House, located on Magazine Street, next to the jail for whites, was the most feared address for blacks in Charleston. Denmark Vesey's later imprisonment and trial would occur there. White masters who so desired could send their slaves with a ticket to the Work House, where for a fee the black would be whipped. This large wooden building had served as a sugar warehouse in colonial years, and the building's former use occasioned a local euphemism for a beating. Charlestonian masters often would rebuke a slave by threatening to send the black downtown "for a little sugar."

To white residents, and some visitors, Charleston in the late eighteenth and early nineteenth centuries was a city of remarkable charm and beauty. But the fear behind these racial ordinances signifies that the white charm was like a grin frozen in the face of an anticipated horror. As with George Whitefield's and Hugh Bryan's calls two generations earlier for the city to repent, the fear was of a ferocious black revolt. Slave rebellions in Jamaica and St. Domingue, the latter successful, only increased this anxiety among white Charlestonians.

What was constant fear to the white population was to be future opportunity for Denmark Vesey. Charleston as a metropolis for a potential slave revolt not only contained the largest black population in the United States but also the largest concentrations of black ethnic groups enslaved directly from Africa. White Charlestonians did not simply prefer "saltwater blacks" in general; the city's importing firms frequently requested slave purchases from among particular national or linguistic groups living along Africa's west coast. Angolans, Ibos, or Gambians were thought by white planters to be particularly suited to the South Carolina climate and agriculture. The monthly arrivals at Charleston in cargo holds of hundreds of these blacks of the same national or linguistic groups meant that it was possible, even in slavery, to preserve at least in part an African identity and a memory as free black people. The slave liberator Jemmy, for instance, organized his revolt at Stono River in 1739 by recruiting among Angolan slaves; three generations later, Denmark Vesey found enough willing recruits among second- and third-generation slaves to organize an exclusively Ibo company within his rebel army.

The growing and covert Africanization of the city was everywhere in evidence for Denmark Vesey to have seen during his two decades as a slave at Charleston, from 1783 to 1800. For example, the distribution of food within the city was de facto controlled by slaves, who either delivered foodstuffs to the city's market or were sent there to shop for households. White Charlestonians throughout the eighteenth century complained that blacks "at their pleasure" chose to "supply the town with fish or not," and that African-American slaves "monopolize the market business" in the city's shopping district. The city's market for foodstuffs must have been, in fact, a frightening place for any white Charlestonian to enter. Located on a slight rise of land above the Cooper River, the former market buildings in the twentieth century have become the popular site of shopping boutiques for tourists. But a white visiting the market in the late eighteenth and early nineteenth centuries would have found its interior arcades peopled almost exclusively by African slaves, conducting business independently without white supervision, and conversing in impenetrable—and, therefore, vaguely disturbing—languages.

Denmark Vesey would have been present in the laboring crowds. One of those residents selected in 1793 to oversee the financing and construction of a market building was Captain Joseph Vesey, owner of a skilled carpenter slave. Three decades later, Denmark Vesey chose the market area as the gathering point for one of his armed companies on the night of his 1822 rebellion.

Among the diversity of African nationalities, languages, and religions flowing around Denmark Vesey, and the black majority at the market and in the streets of Charleston, were the Arabic language and the Islamic faith. The expansion of Islam into central and southwestern Africa in the eighteenth and nineteenth centuries had coincided with the rise of the European and North American slave trade, and Islamic captives also were in the cargo holds of white slavers. The escaped slave Charles Ball, a native of Maryland who wrote a memoir of his South Carolina slavery in 1806, noted the "great many" Africans he had met during his bondage in South Carolina, and that "I knew several who must have been, from what I have since learned, Mohamedans [*sic*]." The percentage of slaves at least nominally Muslim imported from Africa to the great trading centers such as Charleston has been estimated at 10 percent of the total number brought in during the years 1711 to 1808. Proportionately, approximately 8,800 of these Muslim individuals must therefore have been sold in the South Carolina market in these years. In his decades both as a slave and as a freeman, Denmark Vesey almost certainly knew or observed fellow blacks who continued to practice Islam in their bondage.

Vesey's own relationship with, or sympathies toward, Islam remain unknown. The evidence is both inconclusive and intriguing; it is not simply that the Koran teaches that the emancipation of slaves is a virtuous act, or that testimony at his trial established that Vesey, in apparent accordance with Islamic practices and teaching, accepted polygamy and scorned those blacks who drank intoxicating beverages. The date of Vesey's planned revolt, July 14, 1822, also has religious significance. He probably chose that date because, among other reasons, it was a moonless night and also the anniversary of the storming of the Bastille during the French Revolution. But the number fourteen, according to Islamic numerology, is particularly propitious, as representative of the Prophet's name; and the date of July 14, 1822, reckoned by the Islamic lunar calendar, marked the last two months of that Islamic year, Dhu al-Qa'dah and Dhu al-Hijah, respectively. The latter month, Dhu al-Hijah, by which time Vesey had hoped to have liberated his people and to have returned them to Africa, takes its name from the *Hijrah* in the Koran, meaning "to migrate, withdraw, or to make an exodus."

The question of whether he personally professed Islam or the Christianity of his masters was carried unanswered to the grave by Denmark Vesey. However, it is chronologically and geographically possible that during his formative years as a revolutionary, Vesey met and talked with the most extraordinary Muslim slave in South Carolina history. If so, some of the gunfire directed at whites during Vesey's subsequent 1822 revolt could have been a result of his meeting and talking with the remarkable slave known as Omar Ibn Said.

Ibn Said, during his three years' enslavement at a plantation outside Charleston, managed to keep possession of a copy of the Koran, to pray according to Islamic practice, and, eventually, to escape and write his autobiography, which was translated into English. In his memoir, Ibn Said recounted how he had been captured by a raiding party of fellow Africans, sold to white slavers, and carried across the ocean "to a place called Charleston in the Christian language."

Ibn Said related how he was subsequently sold in the Charleston market "to a small, weak and wicked man, named Johnson, a complete infidel, who had no fear of God at all." This master most probably was Archibald Johnson, owner of an extensive plantation at Parker's Ferry, located a few miles outside of Charleston and near the village of Dorchester. Determined to escape "from the hand of Johnson," Ibn Said successfully fled in 1810, and in his freedom he became more fluent in English, being already literate in Arabic and a native speaker of his African language of Futa. In his autobiography, Ibn Said repeatedly urged his readers to "believe on Him who dwells in Heaven, who has sent you a prophet, and you shall understand what a teacher He has sent you."

The paths of Denmark Vesey and this proselytizing Muslim slave may well have crossed. One of Captain Vesey's first investments on settling at Charleston in 1783 had been to lease a lot for construction in Dorchester, a few miles north of Parker's Ferry, and the nearest settlement to the Johnson plantation. In the decades following the Revolution and the early Federal period, the village of Dorchester underwent a building boom, and Denmark Vesey, both as a slave and as a free carpenter, would have had occasion to travel frequently in the area. Whether he met surreptitiously with Omar Ibn Said before the latter's escape in 1810 is historically buried, perhaps intentionally by both men. But what is verifiable is that the Parker's Ferry area later became a site of fierce violence during Vesey's attempted 1822 revolt, with armed blacks firing upon whites attempting to cross the ferry to Charleston.

Thus, by the opening decade of the nineteenth century, the forces necessary for a major slave revolt in South Carolina had come together after two centuries, by either historical chance or historical inevitability, in the person of Denmark Vesey. He was a black man of great physical presence, strength, and intellect, able to grasp the demographic and strategic significance of a black majority in the state, and linguistically fluent and politically facile enough to mold various African ethnic and religious groups into one unified fighting force. From the discipline of Islam he probably took the moral certitude of absolute military victory over unbelievers, just as from an Africanized Christianity he later publicly took the role of a black messianic deliverer. Among those potential black recruits who believed neither in Christianity nor in Islam, Vesey was cunning enough to encourage an African-based Obeah religion, in which belief in an animistic spiritual world guaranteed success for a black uprising against the white masters. And, as a black who had survived the brutalities of slavery in the New World, Vesey was mature enough to wait until the right moment to strike in order to have a chance for victory.

Denmark Vesey had passed from adolescence to mature manhood in servitude, being approximately thirty-two years old in 1799. Occasionally, he apparently had a little money of his own, as the Charleston city government tolerated the practice of slaves' "hiring out" their labor for wages with the permission of their owners, and it was sometimes possible with guile to withhold sums from one's master. On a date somewhere around December 9, 1799, Denmark Vesey bought a ticket in the East Bay Street lottery. The offices were located only a few blocks from the city market, and close by Charleston's docks for the arrival of slave ships. Vesey bet on number 1884.

Whether this number was as arbitrary as Denmark Vesey's fate as a slave, or whether it had a religious significance for him within the long tradition of Muslim numerology, is not known. It is perhaps of significance that the first, eighth, and fourth letters respectively of the Arabic alphabet spell a word of significance in the Islamic faith, rendered as *add-th* in English. In this vowelless alphabet, these letters can represent the word *(h)ad-d(i)th*, one of various sayings of the Prophet repeated after performing obedience to Allah. A frequent *haddith* among devout Muslims is "God is with those who have patience."

By early in the year 1800, Denmark Vesey was informed that he held the winning lottery ticket. He received $1500, enough to buy his freedom out of slavery in this "place called Charleston in the Christian language."

CHAPTER THREE

The African Church and Denmark Vesey as Prophet

. . . Christian nations have not done all they might, or should have done, on a principle of Christian benevolence, for the civilization and conversion of the Africans.

—Dr. Richard Furman,
South Carolina Baptist Convention,
Of the Views of the Baptists, Relative to the
Coloured Population in the United States, *1823*

He was the first to rise up and speak, and he read to us from the Bible, how the Children of Israel were delivered out of Egypt from bondage.
—Rolla Bennett, testifying against Denmark Vesey, 1822

FROM THE PURCHASE of his freedom from slavery in 1800 until his execution by the city of Charleston in 1822, Denmark Vesey was, legally, a human being. As a freed black, he was both financially and socially elevated above the anonymous crowds of slaves in Charleston's streets, and, in the terminology of the late twentieth century, he became "mainstream," or a bourgeois black. Vesey owned, or at least rented, a house at 20 Bull Street, located within three blocks of the private residences of both the governor of South Carolina and the mayor of Charleston. He became a member of the Second Presbyterian Church, one of the city's most prominent houses of Christian worship. Yet, as in his twentieth-century portrait, Denmark Vesey deliberately and inexplicably turned his face away from the mainstream of other freed blacks in nineteenth-century Charleston. He began by the second decade of his freedom to attend the African Methodist Episcopal (A.M.E.) Church, an exclusively "colored" congregation that emphasized distinctively African forms of worship. He deliberately alienated himself from the largely accommodationist mulatto society of free persons of color then residing in Charleston. He became a messianic, and publicly vocal, opponent to black slavery. And by early 1818, for reasons apparently unrelated to his personal security or circumstances, Denmark Vesey began organizing the largest slave revolt in U.S. history.

Vesey purchased his freedom in 1800 with $600 of his lottery winnings. Significantly, Captain Joseph Vesey was under no legal obligation to sell Denmark Vesey his freedom, even if the slave was privately well off. In fact, there were good business reasons for the Captain not to release his slave from a lifetime of bondage. A skilled slave carpenter hired out by his master could earn an average wage of one dollar a day for his owner. The captain could have realized at least $200 within a year and still have retained possession of a skilled slave who could continue to be hired out in future years for additional profits.

Why, then, did Captain Vesey sell freedom to Denmark Vesey? Human slavery is at bottom an ambiguous business: a mixture of economic cruelty, physical dominance, the desire to be feared or admired, and unavoidable moments of intimacy. The slave is both an "I-It" and an "I-Thou," both a person and not a person, as Joseph Vesey must have had occasion to learn during the seventeen years that Denmark Vesey had been his property in Charleston. Indeed, Captain Vesey's historical records imply, for a man of his background, an interesting intimacy and tolerance toward people of color. During his first decade of residence at Charleston, the federal census recorded a notably high number of free persons of color living in Captain Vesey's household—four free people of color as well as eight slaves in 1790—and the captain on occasion acted as a legal patron for free blacks named Vesey outside his household, enabling them to hold property and to make wills. The captain may have done the same for Denmark Vesey, facilitating the way for this black man to take up residence at 20 Bull Street, and selling his former slave his freedom for a generously low price. It is possible, of course, that Captain Vesey simply needed the ready cash in 1800: In the following decade, he would be taken to court seven times for late payment of his debts. In any case, after purchasing his manumission, Denmark Vesey was left with $900 to start him in his freedom. Compared with other slave masters, Captain Joseph Vesey was not a bad sort, especially for a former "Guinea captain," or slave merchant.

For the following decade, 1800–1810, Denmark Vesey lived prosperously and obscurely as a freed black carpenter. But after the revelation of his plot and his execution in 1822, the question arose as to why this supposedly peaceful tradesman became a violent revolutionary between 1810 and 1822. A popular belief in Charleston throughout the last half of the nineteenth century was that his motivations were exclusively personal and domestic. Denmark Vesey was reported to city officials as having said before his attempted revolt that "he was satisfied with his own condition, being free; but, as all his children were slaves, he wished to see what he could do for them."

But, again, when the extant documents are examined, the personal history of Denmark Vesey remains an enigma, and the facts of his life are contradictory or lost. During the years of his freedom, Vesey acknowledged several sons, but not all were slaves. One was described by a Charleston slave as a stout "black fellow" who "looked very much like Denmark, had a full face, and he could read." This son almost certainly was Robert Vesey, who may have been born free as the son of Denmark Vesey and a free black woman. (Robert Vesey later became a prominent builder and practical architect in Charleston.) The mother of Robert Vesey may have been Susan Vesey, who was recorded by the city of Charleston as a free woman of color living at 20 Bull Street in 1822. Although the last name may indicate simply that she was another former slave of Captain Vesey to whom he had given or sold freedom, it is more probable that Susan and Denmark cohabited on Bull Street as free husband and free wife.

Whatever ideological, religious, or political conversions Denmark Vesey may have experienced from 1810 to 1822, they were not likely to have been motivated exclusively by the legal state of his children or wives. Nor was he a mulatto, as several nineteenth-century historians insisted, implying that European cunning became consanguineous with African savagery in this man. In court records, Denmark Vesey, despite his literacy and his multifluency, is consistently described as a freed *black* man. In fact, Vesey probably saw nineteenth-century Charleston's sizable population of freed mulatto citizens as his class enemy, and he rightly judged them as presenting the greatest danger of betrayal of his planned slave revolt.

During the two decades of Vesey's residence as a free man, Charleston tolerated 1,475 free people of color, a little under 6 percent of the city's population from 1810 to 1820. Many of them were mulattoes, and frequently they were the illegitimate sons and daughters of white masters and female slaves. These offspring had been manumitted in personal wills or special acts of the legislature as "favorite" or "especially deserving" servants worthy of freedom. The mulatto elite therefore enjoyed connections through kinship, family financing, or social occasions to the slaveholding whites of Charleston. Since pre–Revolutionary War decades, a social tradition in Charleston had been annual "balls given by Negro and Mulatto women to which they invite the white gentlemen." The white gentlemen also provided financial backing to the freed mulatto community. During the lifetime of Denmark Vesey, the hotel considered the most refined in Charleston was owned by Jehu Jones, a free mulatto, and the governor of South Carolina insisted upon giving Jones's hotel the patronage of his administration. Nor did the mulatto elite disagree with their white patrons on the question of black slavery. A free mulatto woman, one of Vesey's neighbors, bought a twelve-year-old female slave for $300 in 1822. And within a few paces of Vesey's residence, Robert Smyth, a free mulatto carpenter who lived at 15 Bull Street, possessed six slaves in 1820.

Even the question of slavery was effectively nol-prossed by the Brown Fellowship Society, the exclusive social and benevolence club founded by Charleston's mulatto elite in 1790, which forbade the discussion of "religion or politics" at the society's meetings. Despite his earnings and his respectable address from 1810 to 1822, there is no evidence that Denmark Vesey ever was invited or accepted membership into the Brown Fellowship Society.

The mulatto elite also distanced themselves from the place of Christian worship where free blacks and many of the slave majority congregated. Denmark Vesey later made this distinctively black church the site of recruitment for his planned revolt. Prosperous and free mulattoes preferred to worship with their former white masters at St. Philip's Episcopal Church, founded by the city's original Barbadian slave owners, or at such prestigious white churches as Second Presbyterian, where Denmark Vesey was recorded as a member. (The charter organizers of the Brown Fellowship Society in 1790 all had been communicants at St. Philip's, where they were allowed to attend in segregated pews, although they were not permitted burial in the church's grounds.)

But in 1815, black members of the city's Methodist congregations effectively staged a mass protest against the institutional inequality of Charleston's white churches, and they withdrew their memberships. Under the leadership of a free black man, Morris Brown, these dissidents established the first African Methodist Episcopal church in the city. At first convening in an empty hearse house near a black burial ground on Pitt Street, and then in Cow Alley, the A.M.E. congregation later succeeded in erecting a permanent church building in the Charleston suburb of Hampstead, and gaining 4,367 full- or part-time members. This number on the church's rolls, nearly four times the total number of free persons of color in Charleston, indicates that the A.M.E. congregation drew its members from both the free and the enslaved. Among them was Denmark Vesey, who was chosen as a minister class leader for biblical instruction.

Why did Charleston's white authorities in 1815 tolerate the establishment of the African church, and was Denmark Vesey's move to the congregation motivated by personal belief or political opportunism? The first question is answerable with more certainty. Southern slaveholders had come under increasing criticism early in the nineteenth century by the northern U.S. press and the British-based Society for the Propagation of the Gospel for allowing their slaves to exist in what early abolitionists termed spiritual ignorance. South Carolinians, therefore, who gave permission to their slaves to worship independently at the African church were thereby demonstrating their enlightenment and benevolence as masters; a self-congratulatory tone had long been characteristic of the Charleston ruling class, and these white slaveholders thus became unwittingly a pale reflection of the philosopher John Locke's dream of Carolina as a land of religious freedom and tolerance. And, of course, true to their Barbadian heritage, the Charleston authorities ultimately did not tolerate the African church. In 1817, and again in 1818, the government sent its police force to beat and arrest A.M.E. members, and physically disperse its congregation and destroy the church building.

The depth of Denmark Vesey's religious belief is more unfathomable. From his probable knowledge of Islam and the Koran, Vesey likely had a belief in himself as a "man of the Book," ethically and spiritually superior to other persons, black or white. (The public statement by the prominent white nineteenth-century Baptist Dr. Richard Furman that more needed to be done for the "conversion" of Carolina's blacks in the year after Vesey's revolt is more inferential evidence that Islam or Obeah was currently practiced among the state's slaves.)

But the facts that are known are that Vesey seized upon the structure of the African church by 1817 as the means of organizing and recruiting for his coming revolt; sixteen members of his conspiracy who were hanged and four of his eight principal lieutenants in the planned 1822 revolt were later identified as former members of the A.M.E. church. In his position as class leader in biblical discussion with the enslaved A.M.E. members, Vesey found in the Christian Scriptures, as did the black civil rights leaders of the 1960s, a moral imperative for radical social change. He was enabled to preach an apocalyptic rhetoric that made powerless men willing to fight for their freedom.

"He studied the Bible a great deal," a slave later testified against Vesey at his 1822 trial, "and tried to prove from it that slavery and bondage is against the Bible." Another slave recalled in 1822 how Vesey "read to us from the Bible, how the children of Israel were delivered out of Egypt from bondage." Two scriptural passages that Vesey apparently emphasized frequently, and which his black listeners, under oath, recalled his applying to their bondage at Charleston, were Joshua 6:21 and Zachariah 14:1–2: "And they utterly destroyed all that were in the city, both man and woman, both young and old . . ." and "Behold, the day of the Lord cometh, and thy spoil shall be divided in the midst of thee. For I shall gather all nations against Jerusalem to battle; and the city taken, and the houses rifled, and the women ravished. . . ."

Many listened, and believed, as throughout 1817–1818 Vesey

conducted Bible lessons in slave quarters, or, later, at his Bull Street house. Once, when one slave listener objected to Vesey's implied spiritual arguments for a violent black revolution and a white genocide, Vesey silenced the doubter by stating, simply, "The Lord has commanded it." This prophetic certitude and the sheer physical presence of this free carpenter must have been impressive to his audiences, evoking either their respect or, literally, awe. One slave, later arrested in the conspiracy, told city authorities that even before the conspiracy he had feared Denmark Vesey more than he feared any white master; in fact, the slave declared to astonished authorities, he feared Vesey more than he feared God.

By 1817, Vesey had found as an ally another member of the A.M.E. congregation. This was a man who later would become one of his principal lieutenants in the revolt, and who could speak the language and use the religious symbolism of those among Charleston's slaves who did not profess Christianity, or who practiced a second religion in addition to the white people's Christianity. His name was Jack Pritchard, or, as he was universally known in the Charleston District by both whites and blacks, "Gullah Jack."

Gullah Jack was a native of Angola and, by virtue of his membership in the A.M.E. church, at least nominally a Christian. To white Charlestonians, he was also a familiar, and somewhat comical, sight on the city's streets: a short, bandy-legged man with a pair of outlandish side-whiskers, who "acted the fool" before white people and who was probably not overzealously worked by his owner. Gullah Jack had, in short, perfected a "shuck-and-jive" persona for white observers. They were not aware of the respect, and fear, with which he was regarded by other blacks, particularly among the slaves on Charleston's isolated coastal islands, who were known as the Gullah.

To other blacks, Gullah Jack was "the little man who can't be killed," a shaman who could project his mind into others' bodies, an herbalist skilled in the use of medicines or poisons, and an Obeah-man of great power who could conduct rituals or create amulets to protect one against the white man's bullets. Gullah Jack was held in particular veneration by the coastal island slaves, who had managed to preserve in the New World much of their African culture and religion, and even to African-ize the English language into a distinctive vernacular that was practically impenetrable to any person, black or white, not raised on these islands. Pritchard could speak Gullah and practice their religion, and, as he confided to Vesey, hated whites for their enslavement of him and other blacks. With the confidence of Gullah Jack, Vesey therefore gained not only an important ally in recruiting other rebels from among the A.M.E. rolls but also an instrument in organizing the quasi-Christian blacks and the Gullah island people living outside the perimeters of urban Charleston.

There is no conclusive evidence that Denmark Vesey from 1817 to 1822 ever took into his confidence the Reverend Morris Brown, the free black who had organized the A.M.E. church at Charleston, or that Vesey ever intimated to Brown the insurrec-tionist doctrines Vesey was preaching as a class leader. Although Brown's opposition to slavery was well known and courageous, Vesey apparently did not trust other free blacks or free mulattoes; remarkably few were inducted into his incipient recruitment. Nor did Charleston authorities, until after the fact, realize that Vesey was recruiting for revolt among the A.M.E. congregation. But white suspicion of assemblies of blacks, even for religious purposes, was no less sharp-eyed than during the years of Hugh Bryan's Great Awakening and the Stono Rebellion. A writer to the *Charleston Times* publicly complained in 1816 about exclu-sively African-American congregations: "Almost every night there is a meeting of these noisy, frantic worshippers. . . . Mid-night! Is that the season for religious convocation?" The writer continued:

That the meeting of numerous black people to hear the scripture expounded by an ignorant and (too frequently) vicious person of their own color can be of no benefit either to themselves or the community is certain; that it may be attended with many evils is, I presume, obvious to every reflecting mind.

On December 3, 1817, the city guard raided the African church and arrested 469 blacks in attendance there, charging them with disorderly conduct, "they having bought a lot, erected a building and engaged therein in a species of worship which the neighborhood found a nuisance." The A.M.E. congregation persevered, however, and the next year the city government found it necessary to strike again. On June 9, 1818, a correspondent styled "Patriot" reported to the *Courier* the following news:

One hundred and forty Free Negroes and Slaves, belonging to the *African Church*, were taken up Sunday afternoon by the City Guard, and lodged in the Guard-House. The City Council yesterday morning sentenced five of them, consisting of a Bishop and four Ministers, to one month's imprisonment, or to give security to leave the state. Eight other ministers were also sentenced, separately, to receive ten lashes or pay a fine each of five dollars.

Rev. Morris Brown, who was among those free blacks ordered to leave the state or be imprisoned, bravely chose imprisonment in order to continue in Charleston as pastor of his flock. Denmark Vesey, as a class leader or minister of the A.M.E. church, was almost certainly among those sentenced in 1818 to receive either ten lashes or to pay five dollars. Once again, however, the personal history is buried with Vesey; the records of the city guard and the Work House were either lost or deliberately destroyed for the years 1818–1822, when Vesey became known to police authorities.

What is incontrovertible is that the 1818 police raid in Hampstead was a radicalizing event to many Charleston blacks. In the view of one twentieth-century historian, the only "avenue for self-expression and the growth of a sense of community" among the free and enslaved blacks in Charleston was brutally stripped away when the city police broke down the doors of the A.M.E. building and arrested 143 of the congregation. More directly, and ominously, after news of the raid reached the coastal islands, Gullah Jack sent word to Vesey and other members of the congregation that "the Gullah people were ready" to undertake violent retribution. Vesey counseled restraint; and for the next four years, 1818–1822, he traveled the Charleston District, talking and meeting with blacks living as far as forty or sixty miles from the heart of the city.

Vesey's motives were not peaceful. He was also proselytizing among the rural slaves who labored at the riverine plantations surrounding Charleston, spreading his word of a violent revolution and the inevitable destruction of the South's premier slave city. During these four years, he particularly recruited among plantations along the Santee River, forty miles north of the city, an area that was then known as the French Santee. Although in the twentieth century this area is dotted with recreational lakes and golf resorts with a largely white patronage, the French Santee from 1818 to 1822 was one of the most ethnically and culturally diverse societies in the Middle Atlantic southern states, and a fertile ground for black revolution. Here had settled the French-speaking white planters driven from the island of St. Domingue, later the Republic of Haiti, by the successful black uprising of 1791. South Carolina had been in the forefront of the U.S. states offering resettlement to these white refugees, many of whom brought their French- or Creole-speaking slaves with them. A relief society had been organized at Charleston, and former St. Domingue planters had reestablished their slave enterprises at plantations along the banks of the Santee. Their transported slaves, who became known throughout the Charleston District as the French Negroes, were thus the most numerous group of black people in South Carolina who in the nineteenth century had witnessed a successful slave uprising. Vesey spent much of his time among them from 1818 to 1822.

Vesey could speak French, and he had the common experience with the French Negroes of having survived the St. Domingue sugar fields as a slave, until he had feigned epilepsy and escaped to the sea. In the fall of 1793, St. Philip's Episcopal Church and other of Charleston's white churches had called upon their congregations for donations to aid "the distressed inhabitants" of St. Domingue then arriving in the hundreds at the port city. A relief committee had been appointed by the city government to receive donations and distribute them to the refugee French planters. Captain Joseph Vesey was appointed as the treasurer of this committee. It is more than possible, then, that Denmark Vesey, as a twenty-six-year-old slave living in Captain Vesey's house at 281 King Street, in 1793 had taken advantage of his knowledge of French to speak to the transported St. Domingue slaves in the back hallways and rooms of the captain's house.

From 1818 to 1822, Denmark Vesey also spoke surreptitiously but with certainty to the French Negroes along the Santee River, telling them that the Haitian government would surely send a black army to aid North American slaves if only they would revolt; or, as an alternative, all U.S. black rebels could flee either to Haiti or to Africa after killing their white masters and looting the city of Charleston. Whether the Haitian government ever received any communication from Vesey, or encouraged his plans for revolt, is questionable; but Vesey had built up his personal image as a prophet to the variously enslaved black groups around Charleston.

To the A.M.E. converts, Vesey had presented himself as a messianic Christian who spoke in terms of an Old Testament deliverance of blacks from their bondage. Among the quasi-Christian slaves of the Sea Islands, he was a savage chieftain who, as a token of his powers, had chosen Gullah Jack as his war adviser and his familiar. To the French Negroes, Denmark Vesey, with his commanding intellect, his knowledge of Caribbean slavery, and his fluency in French, was another Toussaint L'Ouverture, the brilliant black political and military leader who had defeated a white army in Haiti.

"Every principle which could operate upon the mind of man was artfully employed," his Charleston judges later wrote of Vesey's conspiratorial activities. "Religion, hope, fear, and deception were resorted to as the occasion required. All were told, and many believed, that God approved of their designs; those whose fears would have restrained them, were forced to yield by threats of death; those whom prudence and foresight induced them to pause, were cheered with the assurance that assistance from Santo Domingo and Africa were at hand. . . . And strange as it may appear, yet vast numbers of the Africans firmly believed that Gullah Jack was a sorcerer; that he could neither be killed or taken; and that whilst they retained the charms which he had distributed they would themselves be invulnerable."

Their accusatory words were not intended as praise for Vesey; even in the formal words of his nineteenth-century accusers, however, there can be found confirmation of his remarkable achievement. Vesey had combined the apocalyptic visions of the white planter Hugh Bryan with the black nationalism of Jemmy and the Stono River rebels; to this rhetoric and sense of negritude, he added the historical example of the successful slave revolt in Haiti and the empowering magic of Gullah Jack in rituals that made male slaves perceive themselves as proud warriors. And this extraordinary change of self-perception among the black population of the Charleston District was accomplished by Denmark Vesey in less than ten years.

But from 1818 to 1822, nothing happened among the Charleston slaves but talk. Despite their outward placidity, however, these were years of crisis both for the Carolina planters and for Denmark Vesey personally. South Carolina was approaching a demographic and economic critical point during those four years, as the slave economy tightened its grip upon white and black people alike, rendering both races more precarious and unstable in their conditions there. Blacks were approaching their greatest majority in the district, at the same time that whites were increasingly unable financially to feed or house their slave population. The time for another black revolt was thus particularly propitious. And to Denmark Vesey, who was approaching his sixtieth year in 1822, it must have been an inescapable reality that he had but a few more active years remaining "to see what he could do for his people."

It was at this juncture in his life that Vesey came more frequently to the attention of Charleston's police authorities. Previously regarded by many of the city's whites as a respectable, if somewhat standoffish, free black carpenter, by the late 1810s he began to act in ways that the city guard would have characterized as typical of a "bad nigger." For example, Vesey started refusing to bow to white pedestrians he encountered when walking down Charleston's palmetto-shaded sidewalks. (This was an expected obeisance which other Charleston blacks considered necessary for survival.) Within hearing of white pedestrians, Vesey would then rebuke those blacks who did bow, declaring that "all men were born equal" and that he himself "would never cringe to the whites, nor ought anyone who had the feelings of a man." Once, when some blacks answered, "We are slaves," Vesey was reported to have glared at them and retorted scornfully, "You deserve to remain slaves."

There were also to be endured the official humiliations and personal harassments that Vesey must have experienced as a free black, which would have become more intolerable as he approached late middle age. Even as a free black, Vesey was not allowed to attend the city's theaters, or to walk in the exclusive peninsular park of White Point after sunset. The city's free mulatto elite documentably shunned him; and although technically permitted to travel at will throughout the state, Vesey was subject on any nighttime journey to detention by the state's militia patrol, at which point he would be forced to produce documents establishing his freedom. All this while there was the additional frustration of knowing, secretly, that a black revolt led by him was at least possible in South Carolina; by one account, he kept lists of the names and locations of slaves who had declared themselves to him as willing to fight for their freedom, and Vesey's lists were said to contain over nine thousand names.

By no later than December 1821, Vesey had recruited at least five principal lieutenants who had among their acquaintances dozens, or perhaps hundreds, of followers and friends who said they were willing to join in a black revolt. All his chief coconspirators were slaves, and their numbers included no mulattoes. Besides Gullah Jack, Vesey's chief lieutenants were Ned Bennett, Rolla Bennett (the identical last names indicate not that Ned and Rolla Bennett were related but that they were the slaves of the same man), Monday Gell, and Peter Poyas.

Ned Bennett was a trusted and beloved slave of South Carolina's then governor, Thomas Bennett, and was later described as a black man of "firm nerves," with such a habitually stoic expression before white people, "it was impossible to discover or conjecture what were his feelings." He had at times been a member of the A.M.E. congregation, and he volunteered to lead the "country people," or non-French-speaking plantation slaves, in revolt. Ned Bennett's fellow slave in the governor's household, Rolla Bennett, was said to be a man of "uncommon self-possession," whom the governor on occasion left in charge of his household. Although he later stated that "the governor treats me like a son," Rolla Bennett volunteered to murder Governor Thomas Bennett and his family on the eve of a slave insurrection. Monday Gell, the third conspirator and a possible weak link in the chain, "enjoyed all the substantial comforts of a free man" and was allowed by his master to keep a substantial amount of the profits from his work as a harness-maker in his shop on Meeting Street. Gell was an African Ibo, had lived in this country for about twenty years, and assured Vesey that he had access to firearms.

Vesey's fourth lieutenant, Peter Poyas, was described at the time of his trial as "a first-rate ship's carpenter" who "wrote a good hand." He had secreted a personal weapon, a sword, and insisted to Vesey that "we are obliged to revolt." In late 1821, Poyas took Vesey aside one day and with evident frustration declared to him, "We cannot go on like this."

Accordingly, by mid-1822, Denmark Vesey had sent Ned Bennett to spread the word to the country people, informing them of the appointed date in July for the revolt; at Vesey's orders, Peter Poyas, Rollo Bennett, and Monday Gell were collecting arms and organizing companies among the A.M.E. congregation, the Ibo, and the French Negroes; and Vesey passed word to Gullah Jack for the people of the Sea Islands to make ready their deepwater boats and their weapons for arrival at Charleston on the same appointed date in July. The revolution had begun.

CHAPTER FOUR

———— ◀◉▶ ————

Nothing Can Be Done Without Fire

> *Slave driver,*
> *Your table is turned;*
> *Catch a fire,*
> *You gonna get burned.*
> *—Bob Marley, "Slave Driver," 1971*

O<small>N A PLEASANT EVENING</small> about the third week in May 1822, approximately one dozen black men made their way individually to Denmark Vesey's house at 20 Bull Street. The last arrived shortly after nine o'clock, and the wooden gate concealing the piazza and the yard of the house from the street was then fastened shut. Despite the citywide curfew for slaves, Charleston's white police guard would not have thought anything remarkable was occurring had they noticed one or two of these slaves enter the house. Vesey was known to employ other blacks to assist him in his carpentry business, and the current practice by many of Charleston's white masters of hiring out their domestic slaves for cash in the economically depressed year of 1822 meant an unusually high number of blacks after sunset on the city streets.

Nor was there anything suspect about Vesey's house. A single-story wooden structure, possibly then painted white, as it is today, the house was a respectable dwelling for a resident of either race in the city. It was sited in typical Charleston fashion, with the narrow end of the building facing the street, thus concealing the entrance and the piazza from public view. The sharply angled wooden roof extending well over the piazza indicated that this was a tradesman's or a mechanic's house, with business conducted in the front yard or front rooms and the private lives of the residents concealed in three smaller rooms at the rear of the house.

The month of May was the most pleasant time of the year in Charleston, a peaceful prelude before the burning heat of summer or the fury of fall's tropical storms. Then, as now, the night streets in the richer residential districts were scented by walled gardens unseen in the darkness, by the expensive perfume of imported jasmine vines or the highly poisonous chocolate-fragrant flowering white oleander. Above the private gardens of the wealthier residents, the steeple of St. Philip's Episcopal Church continued to be darkly visible against the night stars, a reassuring symbol of the power of the city's slaveholding class. Had the city guard that same evening approached Vesey's house for a closer look, they would have seen a humbler, but equally reassuring, scene of black domesticity and docility. Visible in the light through the front windows of the house, as on nights past, were two black women, one of them probably Susan Vesey, ironing clothes. The black men of the house doubtless were repairing tools or discussing carpentry tasks in the back rooms.

Vesey was, in fact, making his final preparations for Charleston's destruction at this meeting with his lieutenants in the back rooms of his Bull Street residence. His original band of five coconspirators—Gullah Jack, Ned and Rollo Bennett, Monday Gell, and Peter Poyas—had been enlarged by late May to at least twenty-nine other active recruiters and respected men from the slave community. Their number included Mingo Harth, Bacchus Hammett, and Batteau Bennett, the latter another domestic slave of Governor Thomas Bennett, and one who swore he would rather murder his master or die violently resisting than continue life even as a privileged slave. For weeks, perhaps months, before that May meeting, these men had approached other blacks surreptitiously on the streets of Charleston or the outlying plantations. The invitations to join in the black revolt in many instances had been worded identically, perhaps at Vesey's insistence. "What news?" the recruiter casually would ask the potential slave rebel. When the response came that there was nothing particularly newsworthy in the lives of blacks at Charleston, the secret recruiter would answer, "We are free." When the slave incredulously asked, "Who makes us so?" the men sent by Vesey would answer with a biblical certainty, "I will show you the man."

By mid-1822, these conversations had been repeated hundreds of times throughout the Charleston District. Not all potential recruits had been taken to Vesey's house to meet him personally, but by that spring and summer Vesey had spoken several times to large gatherings of slaves secretly assembled by his coconspirators at the French Santee and at a plantation on a lightly policed, unincorporated area of the Charleston peninsula known as the Neck. At Vesey's instructions, his coconspirators had kept secret rolls of the names of their recruits, and on his counsel, each conspirator had kept his list separate and away from the eyes of all others. Hence, if Vesey or any of his associates were arrested, those not seized by the authorities could destroy their lists, and possibly save their own lives and those of their slave recruits. Peter Poyas, who was the ship's carpenter who "wrote in a good hand," according to white authorities, and who was an early convert to Vesey's argument for a violent black revolution, claimed to possess a list of six hundred names of slaves willing to fight for their freedom within the Charleston District.

Now, at this meeting with his closest twelve lieutenants, Vesey reviewed assignments for the burning of Charleston preparatory to the slave uprising—for, as Vesey and the others had agreed, "nothing could be done without fire." Monday Gell agreed to hide in his harness shop a keg of gunpowder that Bacchus Hammett had stolen from his master. Another recent recruit, Lot Forrester, had managed to obtain unnoticed a length of "slow match," or fuse, from the South Carolina State Arsenal located on Meeting Street. Forrester had hidden the fuse at a dock frequented by black laborers, where it could readily be retrieved and used to fire incendiaries throughout the city. "The best way for us to conquer the whites is to set the town on fire at several places," Vesey emphasized to his followers, "and for every servant in the yards to be ready with axes, knives, and clubs, to kill every [white] man as he came out when the bells rang."

After outlining this initial panic and slaughter, Vesey demonstrated in his subsequent plans the "great penetration and sound judgment" with which his executioners later credited him. On the same night as Charleston was to be set afire, the city and its stores of weapons were to be attacked simultaneously by columns of armed slaves arriving from the south, the north, and the east. Peter Poyas, who had been a rock of support during Vesey's early talk of revolt, was given the critical assignment of marching from the south into the city with a band of coastal blacks and seizing the state arsenal at Meeting Street and the Guard House; at the same time, a column under Gullah Jack on the Bulkley Farm, north of the city at the Neck, was to seize private weapon shops and join forces with Rolla Bennett's band at the smaller U.S. arsenal there, distribute the firearms, and proceed through the center of the city, killing all white people in their path; meanwhile, companies of Ibo and French warriors were to arrive by canoe at the docks to the east, near the market, and also advance toward the city's center at Meeting Street and the city guard building under the leadership of Bacchus Hammett and Monday Gell; in the residential districts, Ned Bennett was given the task of murdering his master, the governor, as well as the mayor of Charleston, before reuniting his forces with Vesey and his immediate followers two blocks away on Bull Street. Vesey and the others then would complete the concentration of black forces by marching toward the center of the city to join the other columns of armed slaves. While the blacks were thus converging in overwhelming force at the critical center of Charleston, Vesey instructed, smaller bands—draymen, coachmen, hostlers, or any black who might have access to a horse—were "to ride through the streets and kill every [white] person they might meet, and prevent them from assembling or extending the alarm."

Weapons and surprise would be needed if the blacks were to succeed in overcoming the arsenals and distributing firearms to rebel slaves. Pompey Haig, a recent recruit, had informed Vesey earlier of the willingness of "Frenchmen, blacks, very skillful in making swords and spears, such as they use in Africa," to arm the rebels. Now, at this May meeting, Gullah Jack declared his willingness to carry the edged weapons to the Bulkley Farm, a plantation located at the northern end of the peninsula. Another recent recruit, John Vincent, had stolen a bullet mold, and, by this time in May, musket balls had been cast and had been hidden in bags by blacks at locations throughout the city. Nor had Vesey overlooked the element of surprise. In a detail that was later of a particular frisson to whites, Vesey had purchased from an unwitting white barber wigs and false whiskers made from the hair of white people. "[W]ith the assistance of these, and by painting their faces," Vesey's judges later wrote of the black rebels, "they hoped in the darkness of night and in the confusion to be mistaken for white men." The judges continued: "Such a plan as this would no doubt have assisted Peter [Poyas] in his bold determination to advance singly some distance ahead of his party, and surprise and put to death the sentinel before the Guard House."

Many at this meeting already had stolen swords or hunting arms from their masters, and Vesey had arranged for an additional source for edged weapons other than the French Negroes. Vesey announced that he had found a black smithy, hired out by his mistress, who was willing to make secretly one hundred pikes, also to be hidden at the Bulkley Farm. Since this smithy was endangering his livelihood—and his life—by making these weapons under the pretense of seeking jobs outside his mistress's household, Vesey was respectful of the man's safety and labor. At the conclusion of this meeting, he insisted that everyone present contribute twelve and a half cents in order "to pay that black man's wages to his mistress."

The date of Sunday, July 14, 1822, was agreed by all present to be the night of fire and murder. The weapons and companies of men were to be distributed throughout Charleston on that night, and that date provided sufficient time to notify the Republic of Haiti of the possible need for military support and transportation. Once more, Vesey had chosen his date with a particular cunning. In a tradition begun in the Caribbean and accepted in Charleston, blacks were allowed to congregate on Sundays in the city market area with comparatively little supervision; and by mid-July, in a custom also practiced by the city's wealthier white elite, many officers of the militia escaped the summer torpor of the city by vacationing with their families at such northern social centers as Newport, Rhode Island. Hence, the whites in the city would be fewer in number and deprived of many experienced military leaders on the night of revolt.

Vesey also had chosen well by waiting until 1822. That year was perhaps the most critical in the history of the Charleston District—that is, until the firing upon Fort Sumter in 1861—when the slavery system had fastened most tightly upon the port of Charleston, tearing apart blacks and whites in the 1820s in a condition most favorable for violent revolt. Charleston had indulged in an orgy of African slave-buying before the congressionally mandated prohibition of the international slave trade took effect in 1808, and as a result the district's black population had grown exponentially by 1822. At this same time, the international prices for cotton, particularly in the important English market, had plummeted as the newly opened southern frontiers of Alabama and Mississippi began to compete with the established Carolina plantations in producing tens of thousands of bales of low-priced cotton. (In 1818, the price of short-staple cotton peaked at thirty-five cents per pound, and it did not exceed this price until the Civil War.)

As a consequence, Carolina planters were trapped in the economic quandary of having purchased slaves on credit in order to purchase even more slaves on credit. As the market value of their sole cash crop—cotton—decreased almost yearly, the planters covered their cash losses in the only ways they could: by hiring out their slaves or by selling them, regardless of family ties; by reducing the food rations on the plantations; or by increasing the quotas on the gang-labor systems by enforcing longer hours or harsher discipline. Vesey was most likely aware that each of these repressive measures, combined with the burgeoning black majority, was certain to swell his rolls of an estimated nine thousand recruits who had signed their names, or marks, as willing to fight for freedom.

The signs of economic depression—and the increasing white desperation in the slave economy—were everywhere for a literate man such as Denmark Vesey to notice in 1822. The widely circulated *Niles Register*, the national business newspaper of the nineteenth century, noted that year the curious southern phenomenon that although cotton prices worldwide were declining, the region's production of the white staple continued to increase. The editor of the *Register* aptly summarized the trap in which the Carolina planters had caught themselves: "The capital invested [in black slaves] must be employed; and cannot be suddenly and generally changed." Closer to home, the Charleston District planters could extricate themselves partially by selling off their domestics and field hands, despite their oft-repeated platitude that their slaves were "like a family" to them, for whatever cash the market could bring. Typical of the economic stress was an advertisement appearing on May 14, 1822, by the Charleston merchant William Payne, offering "for private sale [a] valuable fellow, a complete House Servant and Carriage Driver, warranted in every respect; sold to raise the money." During the month and a half between the meeting at Vesey's house in May and the scheduled date of the July revolt, the front page of the *Charleston Courier* was filled with columns of these desperate advertisements offering surplus slaves. Each black victim of the sell-off was a potential recruit to Vesey's army.

The economic crisis—and the potential for Vesey's revolt—had been also exacerbated by Charleston's appetite for new slaves two decades earlier. Slave merchants—aware of the deadline of December 31, 1807, after which, according to the U.S. Constitution, the nation's participation in the international slave trade might be proscribed by Congress—had indulged in a final feeding frenzy off the west coast of Africa in the waning months of 1807. Representative of this one-stroke-to-midnight avariciousness was the voyage of the slaver *Commerce,* which set sail from Charleston on June 16, 1807, with instructions from its backers to spend no longer than four months along the African coast before returning to the Charleston market with a full cargo. But by early September, the captain wrote to complain that the African coast was crowded "with no less than 300 sail" of competing ships, that his barter goods "were unsalable" to the black or Arabic slave traders, who could name their own prices, and that he had succeeded in obtaining only eighty-six slaves. However, others of Charleston's "Guinea captains" were much more successful. Between 1804 and 1807, a total of 202 slave ships from Africa docked at Charleston with 26,744 blacks in their cargo holds.

The result was that by 1822, the Charleston District still comprised an extraordinarily large majority of slaves, who were in a perilous condition even by the standards of the gang-labor system. The U.S. census of 1810 had reported a total of 45,385 slaves residing in the Charleston District; in the census of 1820, this number rose to 57,221 slaves to 19,376 whites, an increase of 21 percent in the black population. (What slave masters called a positive "natural increase," or the percentage, usually 2 percent, by which births exceed deaths, accounts for this growth among third-generation American slaves and newly acquired Africans.) To their white owners, this large number of blacks was a drag upon family finances when the price of cotton first began to fall in 1819; to Denmark Vesey, they were potential recruits who were otherwise in danger of racial extinction.

The question in the early 1820s of how to employ these surplus slaves had occupied minds other than Vesey's. The cosmopolitan South Carolina architect Robert Mills, who would later design the Washington Monument (and who in 1822 would improve the Charleston city jail for whites opposite the Work House, where Vesey was to be imprisoned), seriously proposed a Faustian bargain. Just as that mythical damned soul had tried to buy off the devil by promising to reclaim Europe's marshes, so Mills proposed that South Carolina's approximately 47,000 surplus slaves be set to work draining the state's swamps and turning them into "fairy spots" of "delightful habitations."

By 1822, Denmark Vesey had reached a more brutal conclusion: When the population of slaves became effectively unsalable, white masters simply would kill the surplus black human beings. Throughout May and June of 1822, as the scheduled date for the July revolt neared and some recruits expressed second thoughts about slaughtering all the city's whites, Vesey and Peter Poyas repeated to them a rumor with the certitude of fact. Did they not know, Vesey and Poyas asked the wavering recruits, that on a certain date "the whites are going to create a false alarm of fire, and every black that comes out will be killed in order to thin them"?

Vesey probably sincerely believed in this possible genocide of his race. His experiences as an adolescent aboard a slaver had taught him what little value a black life held for a white merchant; and, as he told his recruits in 1822, the whites "would be right to do it," if they only guessed at how much black hatred was directed at the slave empire of Charleston.

As the moonless Sunday night of July 14, 1822, approached, Vesey relentlessly prodded the black population with his three arguments intended to sustain the need for immediate revolt. To the urban members of the former A.M.E. congregation, he emphasized that "our church was shut up so that we could not use it, and that it was high time for us to seek our rights." To the French Negroes, he insisted that "we were fully able to conquer the whites, if we were only unanimous and courageous, as the Santo Domingo people were." And among the Gullahs and the first-generation African slaves, Vesey took particular care, centering upon gatherings of blacks at the Bulkley Farm, to conduct magical rituals of empowerment and cultural identity.

"Vesey was in the habit of going to Bulkley's Farm," a slave later testified in court against him, referring to the plantation at the northern peninsular neck where Gullah Jack had managed to hide spears and pikes. Gullah Jack, in fact, had been holding secret nocturnal gatherings at the Bulkley Farm since at least March 1822, and Vesey probably accompanied him to most of these meetings. Vesey and Gullah Jack brought potential recruits there to meet the slave patriarch of the Bulkley plantation, an African "old daddy," as the other blacks called him, "marked on both sides of his face," probably with tribal scars. The "old daddy" gave the new recruits his blessing. Approximately thirteen to fifty slaves also gathered at these nightly meetings for singing and fasting, and, on one occasion, a participant testified that Gullah Jack brought with him a fowl, and all those present "ate it half raw, as evidence of union." On another occasion, Vesey was walking through the gate of the Bulkley Farm when a large snake suddenly advanced toward him from behind the gatepost. With a grasp of both European wit and sympathetic magic, Vesey killed the reptile, speaking of it as if it were a white man, and then announced to the awed Gullah and Africans, "That's the way we would do it."

At these meetings, Gullah Jack, also under the supervision of Vesey, exercised his own powers as an Obeah-man, or practitioner of sympathetic magic. To the new recruits, Gullah Jack distributed rations of parched corn and ground nuts, with the instructions to "eat that and nothing else on the morning it breaks out; and, when you join us as we pass, put into your mouth this crab-claw, and you can't then be wounded."

For those slaves who were unimpressed by the Bulkley Farm rituals, Vesey and Gullah Jack had another spiritual trump card to play: a blind black man, born with a caul, who lived in the city of Charleston and who "said he possessed a Gift—a species of second sight—which came to him after prayer or in dreams." The judges at Vesey's trial later determined that "the timid and the wavering" among the recruits were brought to this seer's Charleston residence by Vesey, Gullah Jack, or Peter Poyas. There, the blind man would tell the uncertain recruits that he foresaw the rebellion, and told each one "'let not thy heart be troubled, neither be afraid.'"

This unnamed blind man later avoided imprisonment or hanging by insisting to the judges that Vesey had never actually told him of the planned insurrection; rather, like the prophet Hugh Bryan a century before, he testified that in his dreams he independently "had foreseen something of that sort," then had merely repeated a biblical comfort to his frightened visitors. But some slaves remained deeply frightened after these meetings. Harry Haig, later condemned to hanging for his part in the conspiracy, told his judges after his sentencing that Gullah Jack had "charmed" him into joining Vesey's revolt. Although this statement was almost certainly an attempt in part to mitigate his actions and therefore possibly receive mercy, Haig spoke of his conversion by Gullah Jack in terms of psychological oppression. "I felt as if I was bound up," Haig told his judges after Gullah

Jack had worked his rituals on him, "and had not the power to speak one word [to the whites] about it."

Vesey himself had a coldly rationalist view of arson and murder—"they would be right to do it"—and he probably had little personal belief in sympathetic magic. But what is incontrovertible is that these rituals had a profound effect upon the minds of the white population when these meetings became known during Vesey's trial. In sentencing the convicted conspirators, the judges considered proof of any slave's attendance at the Bulkley Farm rituals as prima facie grounds for his hanging.

As the local meetings continued "underground" throughout May 1822, Vesey did not neglect his larger strategy of claiming military aid from the Republic of Haiti. He had insisted since the beginning of his plot in 1818 that, once the night of murder and arson was accomplished at Charleston, the slave army must also be prepared "to take every ship and vessel in the harbor, and to put every man to death except the captains." He instructed his followers that "as soon as they had all the money out of the banks and all the goods out of the stores," the slave army with their black families and a few white female captives must "sail for Santo Domingo, for he had a promise they would receive and protect them."

There is no evidence that Vesey ever received such a pledge from the Republic of Haiti. It is possible, however, that at his instruction a letter had been sent by late winter or early spring of 1822 to President Boyer of Haiti. Monday Gell, who turned state's evidence after his arrest, testified that at Vesey's orders Gell had carried such a letter to give to a black cook aboard a Charleston ship bound for Port-au-Prince, who promised to show the message to Boyer. The letter, Gell confessed to the court, was "about the sufferings of the [Charleston] blacks, and to know if the people of Santo Domingo would help them if they made an effort to free themselves." Gell's testimony was independently corroborated by the confession of coconspirator John

Enslow, who added details that Gell had omitted—that is, that the letter had been written by Gell himself with the assistance of a free African named Prince Graham.

The name of the ship was not identified in the court transcript, and Gell and Enslow disagreed as to which dock in Charleston it was moored at before sailing for Port-au-Prince; but both men were insistent that the letter had been placed aboard the ship no later than the end of March 1822. The *Daily Courier's* "Shipping News" records no ship leaving Charleston Harbor in March or April bound for Port-au-Prince, although vessels did sail from Charleston to the black republic by the end of May. But whether or not Vesey ever actually sent the letter or received a reply, to inspire confidence in his recruits he spoke of Haitian aid as a foregone conclusion. And, as the Charleston blacks were aware, the Bank of the United States was located directly across Meeting Street from the Guard House and the rebels intended to seize it. With the gold specie looted from the bank, Vesey's rebels would be confident of finding a welcome at Port-au-Prince, or many other Caribbean or West African ports.

Thus, either through manipulation, courage, or threats, Denmark Vesey, by May 1822, had organized Charleston's slaves as thoroughly as his hopes allowed "to see what he could do for his fellow creatures." All that remained was to keep the appearance of normality until the slaves would burn and loot the city on July 14. Vesey had strictly commanded his conspirators that "they should assume the most implicit obedience" to their white masters until the night that they could murder them; and, to all outward appearances, as the approaching summer solstice lengthened the days from late May to early June, the city of Charleston seemed as placidly secure as ever. The Carolina Coffee House advertised that "A Fine Green Turtle" would be butchered, with "Soup, Steaks, and Fins" for sale to interested families. The usual summer migration was under way as from fifteen hundred to two thousand wealthier residents left the city for cooler climates when daily temperatures began to soar to ninety-eight degrees. The *Charleston Courier* complained that "We have lived for a day or two past in a burning atmosphere. The whole of animated nature suffers, pants, and groans under these rays. . . ."

Vesey managed during this critical period to keep his organization secret and his coconspirators quiet. Quite bluntly he promised that if any man on the rolls of recruits should betray his plot to the whites, he personally would see to it that the traitor was "put to instant death." He also protected his plot against betrayal by his selective choice of lieutenants and chief recruiters. Although the slaves at Governor Bennett's household were important exceptions, Vesey chose no other domestics, or "house niggers," for inclusion among his important organizers; and he further revealed his inherent distrust of the white-sympathetic elite of mulattoes and free blacks within the city by including among his conspirators only three men later identified by the court as mulattoes.

Peter Poyas agreed to this caution against house servants. This slave carpenter, who had become Vesey's chief disciple, in addressing his own recruits made the point with a vivid image: "But take care and don't mention it [Vesey's plot] to those waiting men who receive presents of old coats from their masters," Poyas emphasized to his recruits, "or they'll betray us. *I* will speak to them."

But on the afternoon of Saturday, May 25, 1822, Peter Prioleau, a house slave of Colonel and Mrs. John C. Prioleau, was leisurely fulfilling an errand for his mistress near the city's wharves when he was approached by another black who was a stranger to him. This slave asked Peter Prioleau whether he had heard "something serious was about to take place." When the house servant replied that he had not heard any particular news, the stranger, who was later identified as William Paul, replied with an answer shocking to Prioleau: "Why, we are determined to shake off our bondage, and for this purpose we stand on a firm foundation. Many have joined, and if you go with me, I will show you the man, who has the list of names, who will take yours down."

Horrified, Prioleau broke off the conversation. But, as he later told the court, he could not "remain easy under the burden of such a secret." That same afternoon, Prioleau sought out the advice of a friend, a free black named William Pencil. Pencil listened, and then this free black urged Prioleau immediately to inform his master of the plot.

CHAPTER FIVE

———◦◉◦———

Theater of Terror: The Magnolia Curtain and the Sable Curtain

[Elias Horry, incredulously]: "Tell me, are you guilty? For I cannot believe unless you tell me so—what were your intentions?"

[John Horry, slave of Mr. Horry]: "To kill you, rip open your belly, and throw your guts in your face."
> —*Recorded dialogue between slave and master, Charleston, July 1822*

THE HOME OF James Hamilton, Jr., Charleston's intendant, or mayor, was located at Cumming and Bull streets, two blocks from Denmark Vesey's residence. On the night of Friday, June 14, 1822, from nine o'clock onward, the intendant's house was ablaze with light as prominent white citizens hurriedly came and went and various senior officers of the state militia arrived to confer with Hamilton.

Hamilton was acting on the sudden confirmation of the warning about a slave revolt given two weeks earlier by the slave Peter Prioleau. Prioleau, on the advice of his free black friend, had informed his master, Colonel John Prioleau, about the disturbing conversation at the city's wharves with a fellow slave, who told him that "something serious was about to take place." Colonel Prioleau heard his slave's story on May 30, and he wasted no time. By three o'clock that afternoon, Peter Prioleau had repeated the tale at the intendant's residence to an audience that also included Governor Thomas Bennett and members of the Charleston City Council. The colonel, meanwhile, on his own initiative, had determined that the appearance of the unknown black recruiter matched the description of a slave in the city, William Paul. Paul was arrested, and on May 31, he was placed into the "black hole" of the solitary confinement cell at the Work House.

Paul initially claimed ignorance of any insurrectionist plot, but within twenty-four hours of his confinement, he began to make the first of several confessions. His captors' means of coercion were not recorded, but they can be readily visualized. A foreign visitor to Charleston in the mid-1820s who dropped in on the Work House later wrote that "order was maintained" by overseers "armed with cowhides." (The cowhide was a common southern frontier weapon, and not to be confused with the lesser cruelty of the bullwhip. When swung by its tapering end toward a human victim, the cowhide both stripped off the skin and bruised the exposed muscle tissue underneath.)

During interrogations that lasted until June 8, Paul told his captors everything he knew about the plot. "Beginning to fear that he would be led forth to the scaffold for summary execution," in the later words of his interrogators, Paul confessed "he had known for some time about the plot, that it was very extensive, embracing an indiscriminate massacre of the whites." Peter Poyas, Mingo Harth, and Ned Bennett were named by the terrified Paul as being among the chief recruiters. All he knew about one of the leaders was that this man was reputed to be a sorcerer, "who carried about him a charm, which rendered him invulnerable."

But, despite the shock of Paul's first confession, the Charleston authorities chose to do very little until the meeting at Intendant Hamilton's house on June 14. Immediately after Paul's confession, Poyas and Harth were questioned at the Work House, but each was released after being held a few hours, and neither was beaten. (William Paul continued to be held in the black hole at the prison.) For white observers, the outlandish little figure of Gullah Jack was not identified with the black sorcerer who Paul claimed was one of the revolt's chief organizers. And, incredibly, even though Paul had been arrested at Denmark Vesey's house, Vesey himself was not considered a suspect in the rebellion by city authorities until much later in June.

This inactivity during the first two weeks of June was partially due to the reluctance of whites to believe that blacks were capable of organized revolt. The initial calm also was the result of the benevolence—or psychological obtuseness—of Governor Bennett toward a black population he considered to be loving toward their white masters. But largely the buying of two weeks' more time for Vesey's revolt was the result of the remarkable performances by three of his closest conspirators before a white audience at the Work House.

The governor was disinclined to believe the whole affair. If the suspected slave insurrectionists included Ned Bennett, the governor told the intendant and other prominent citizens, this entire rebellion was nonsense. Ned Bennett's "attachment and fidelity" to his master was unquestionable, the governor said; and he offered as further proof the fact that "this Negro had been twice in the Northern states" traveling in attendance on the governor, and had refused inducements by agitators there to abandon his master and live free in the North.

The comportment of Peter Poyas and Mingo Harth seems to have confirmed the governor's opinion. Both had been questioned on May 31 at the Work House; but "these fellows behaved with so much composure and coolness, and treated the charges against them with so much levity," their interrogators later wrote, that both were released that same day. Poyas in particular successfully laughed off any revolutionary activity attributed to him as simply misinterpretations of his attempts to proselytize for a new church in his neighborhood.

But it fell to Ned Bennett, the governor's trusted house servant, to deceive the whites most successfully during the critical first two weeks of June. Bennett voluntarily appeared at the Work House on June 12. He explained to the astonished wardens there that he had heard from the governor that his name had been mentioned in relation to a suspicious affair and that he wished to be questioned in order to clear his reputation.

Ned Bennett, a "man of firm nerves" in the opinion of all who knew him, displayed great plausibility during his voluntary interrogation at the Work House, denying any involvement in an insurrectionist plot, and even denying to the whites that such a plot could exist, for as the governor's slave he surely would have heard rumors of it from his fellow blacks. Ned Bennett's composure, combined with the governor's previous declarations of faith in his household slaves, convinced the wardens and the intendant that there was nothing in Paul's talk of a black rebellion, except perhaps the prattling of a mind under torture. Bennett was allowed to leave the Work House unharmed and no longer under suspicion, and the wardens and intendant agreed among themselves by June 12 that there was "no confirmation of the disclosures of William."

But by the end of that same day, Ned Bennett would be meeting with Vesey at his Bull Street house in order to advance the date of the revolt before the whites learned any more of it. Before offering himself for interrogation, Bennett surely had realized that the ultimate success of the revolt, and his escape from torture and the gallows, depended upon the performance he would give at the Work House. His own life hanging in the balance, and contemplating the murder of his master and his master's family, Bennett that June day lost himself among the anonymous crowds of blacks in the streets of Charleston, as accomplished a performer as any white actor in the city's Dock Street Theatre.

THE IMAGE OF THEATER is central to understanding the relation between whites and blacks at Charleston during Vesey's revolt. The city's original Barbadians were at least forthright in their assumption that the slave population would murder its masters if given only half a chance, and that any incipient black resistance must be met with an unhesitating brutality by the white authorities. But by the fifth generation of masters and slaves in South Carolina, a new social relation was beginning to be mutually scripted between blacks and whites at Charleston, one highly complimentary to masters and valuably expedient to slaves. Masters perceived themselves as benevolent but firm parents, ordained by God to direct the errant energies of a childish black race. Blacks found physical safety in their role as a feckless but lovable people, who instinctively turned to Master for guidance in any task more complicated than picking cotton.

This "domestic charade" was, in the phrasing of William Freehling, like "a long-running play" in nineteenth-century Charleston. Each race defined itself toward the other in terms of its role, and each found security in the stereotypical exchanges of their scripted lines. Whites felt safe, and refrained from state violence, as long as they could maintain a Magnolia Curtain, their shared assumption that slaves *would not* revolt because they knew they were loved as an extended black family. (An instance is the well-publicized opinion of Governor Bennett: The kindly treated black slave will refuse freedom, even while accompanying Master on necessary trips to the unfriendly North, in order to return home to the South and abide by the side of the white man he loves.) Blacks found security, and avoided physical retribution, by playing their role of a people who *could not* revolt, whose mature emotions were secretly hidden from harm behind a Sable Curtain of pretended childish incomprehension or simple docility.

Probably thousands of whites and blacks in Charleston had, until the summer of 1822, maintained the Magnolia Curtain and the Sable Curtain with utmost sincerity. Governor Bennett, who was a comparatively humane slave master, truly did not believe, until Vesey's revolt was practically at his doorstep, that Ned or Rolla Bennett would *really* cut his benevolent master's throat. Peter Prioleau and William Pencil truly were distressed to learn of the planned rebellion, and their immediate response had been to shirk responsibility and to make their discovery "white folks' business." And doubtless other thousands of blacks deliberately had used their scripted roles to evade white suspicion, and to confirm to whites the perception of black people as harmless children.

But such a racial charade could ensure peace in Charleston only as long as all the actors, in Freehling's phrase, "are one with their act." The whites, for their part, continued until late in June to uphold their role of regarding black revolt as privately unthinkable and publicly unmentionable. The temporary arrests of Peter Poyas and Mingo Harth, and the continued incarceration of William Paul, were explained by the gossip throughout the city that "the boys had been taken up for stealing." (How typical, the white actors could assure one another publicly as they gathered on Meeting Street or Queen Street. Our "boys," however loyal, are as easily tempted to steal as children are to filch sweetmeats. With such a childlike people, one must be firm but forgiving.)

But during the second week of June—while Ned Bennett was meeting with others in emergency council at Vesey's house—there were disturbing public incidents that might have made some white actors pause and wonder what really might be concealed behind the Sable Curtain. Two male adolescents—one black and the other mulatto—were overheard in the street boasting that Charleston's powder magazines were to be exploded and all the white residents murdered. The two boys were sent to the Work House to be whipped for their impertinence, but from what adults had they heard of such an idea? Equally puzzling, "Gullah Jack" Pritchard, who his master now recalled was regarded by other slaves as a "doctor or conjurer," suddenly shaved off his side-whiskers. Master Pritchard was astonished; he knew that these oversized whiskers were Gullah Jack's pride, and that they made him recognizable among Charleston's slave population.

If there was a growing sense of unease behind the Magnolia Curtain during the early summer of 1822, there was also an accumulating rage behind the Sable Curtain. Few situations are as enraging as daily to act submissively when it is not one's true role—to act as a "boy" or a "wench," when in reality one is a man, a woman, or a revolutionary warrior. Vesey strictly had commanded his followers that, until the moment they all could strike a deadly blow, "they should assume the most implicit obedience"; but some of his recruits by the summer of 1822 could forbear no further from tearing down the Sable Curtain and at last shouting out their true feelings to the whites—even if the sure consequences were a trip to the Work House and the gallows.

An instance was the arrest and trial of John Horry. Horry, who according to other slaves' testimonies had stolen a sword and had sworn that on the night of Vesey's revolt he "would go upstairs and kill his master and family," escaped detection until July 5, well after the date when Vesey's revolt had become widely known among whites. Even then, according to a contemporaneous white source, "when the constables came into Mr. Horry's yard to take up his waiting man," the slave's master, Elias Horry, insisted "they were mistaken, that he could answer for [John's] innocence, that he would as soon suspect himself." Elias Horry attended his slave's later trial at the Work House, and, upon hearing the state's evidence, plaintively asked his waiting man: "Tell me, are you guilty? For I cannot believe unless I hear you say so. . . . What were your intentions?" To which John Horry, the Sable Curtain at last torn aside, answered, "To kill you, rip open your belly, and throw your guts in your face." (John Horry was hanged on July 12, 1822.)

But between June 14, when Intendant Hamilton at last realized that he had been deceived about Vesey's revolt, and the end of that month, when mass arrests of suspected slaves began, the majority of whites and blacks at Charleston continued to play the charade of the Magnolia Curtain and the Sable Curtain. In the meantime, however, Denmark Vesey, who remained unarrested and unsuspected until late June, was doing his behind-the-scenes best to bring this drama to a sudden and violent ending: the murder of the entire white audience, and the burning of the urban theater that was Charleston.

VESEY HAD NOT been idle since William Paul's arrest on May 30, nor did he believe for a moment the widely accepted explanation that the city guard was apprehending his conspirators on minor charges of stealing. Within forty-eight hours of Paul's arrest, Vesey had met with Jesse Blackwood, a light-skinned slave who possibly could elude the patrols at night. He told Blackwood to keep himself in immediate preparedness to travel among the rural slaves. Also, on June 1, he spoke with Lot Forrester, the slave who had stolen a length of fuse to explode gunpowder, and told him to come to a meeting at Bull Street on June 12.

By June 9, Vesey was taking the necessary steps to advance the date of revolt before the whites learned any further details. He chose midnight, June 16, of the following weekend, also a "market" Sunday, when blacks could congregate in the city without suspicion. On June 10, he dispatched Frank Ferguson, a trusted conspirator, to spread the word among rural blacks of the new, advanced date, and to tell those slaves "They must come to town and assist."

On June 12, Ferguson met with Vesey, Blackwood, Poyas, Ned Bennett, Monday Gell, and possibly others at Vesey's house. Ferguson reported a "fine success" in rousing the rural blacks. All agreed that Blackwood should be sent into the country to bring more slave soldiers to Charleston on June 16, and a collection of two dollars was taken up in Vesey's back room in order for Blackwood to hire a horse. Blackwood promised to leave that night for St. John's Parish, south of the city.

In fact, Blackwood did not depart until early Sunday morning, June 16, the day of the planned attack. The delay proved, in the end, fatal to him, as well as to Vesey and many other conspirators. In part, Blackwood was held up by his not being able to find a horse for rent until the following weekend; and, partially, this severing of communications was due to the white authorities at last realizing that there was more to the rumored slave rebellion than just talk, and that the Sable Curtain concealed more than just occasional black sullenness.

The final tearing of the Sable Curtain was the act of a mulatto slave. His master, Major John Wilson, was politically ambitious and wished to succeed Governor Bennett, whom he apparently held in low regard for his being so trustful of the city's slaves. Acting independently, Wilson summoned his family's mulatto slave the first week of June; the major instructed the slave, George Wilson, to inquire among blacks in the city whether they had heard any talk of a planned insurrection.

George Wilson did as he was told. He was directed by his master to be particularly inquisitive among the black Methodists of the city, as Major Wilson remembered that denomination as the precursor of the lately destroyed African Church. George Wilson was a class leader of other slaves attending the Independent Congregational Circular Church at Charleston, and he also was apparently trusted by the black Methodists of the city. In these capacities, he was able to draw out the confidences of other people of color.

Late in the afternoon of June 14, George Wilson hurried home with disturbing news for his master. Wilson had been confidentially solicited to join the coming revolt, he told the major, by a black member of the Methodist congregation. (Although purposely unidentified in official reports, this member probably was Mingo Harth.) There was a breathless urgency to the words that George Wilson was reported having told his master: "that the fact was really so, that a public disturbance was contemplated by the blacks and that not a moment should be lost in informing the constituted authorities, as the succeeding Sunday, the 16th, at twelve o'clock at night, was the period fixed for the rising."

Major Wilson lost no time in informing the man he considered the proper authority—not Governor Bennett, but Intendant James Hamilton. By eight in the evening, Major Wilson was at Hamilton's house repeating this latest revelation. It provided to Hamilton sufficient corroboration to the statements by the house servant Peter Prioleau and the imprisoned William Paul. Hamilton was a thin-featured, Scots-Irish politician who was also ambitious to succeed Bennett, and who had married into the Charleston aristocracy with remarkable financial success. (On acquiring a wife, Hamilton also had received from her family the ownership of three plantations and about two hundred slaves.) Thus, on hearing this latest evidence, he acted decisively to protect Charleston's slave-owning class.

Hamilton immediately sent word to Governor Bennett's house, whereupon he received authorization for the captains of the state militia to be summoned to the intendant's residence that same night. There, the military and the intendant agreed between themselves that approximately four hundred of the state militia, including hussar horsemen armed with heavy sabers and pistols, would reinforce the city guard on Sunday night. The city watch force, usually armed only with truncheons, was to be issued firearms, and approximately 16,000 ball cartridges and 300 muskets were to be made ready at the State Arsenal under a strengthened guard. It was also apparently agreed at this meeting that the Charleston authorities would not issue a public alarm to the whites, nor a general warning to the city's blacks. The latter, of course, would continue to be watched extremely closely. Hamilton, in fact, had been particularly suspicious of Peter Poyas and Mingo Harth ever since they had been detained at the Work House. Despite their release from the Work House on May 31, Hamilton had hired spies "of their own color" to follow Poyas and Harth, and "to give advices of all their movements."

Thus two separate dramas were enacted less than two blocks apart on the Friday evening of June 14. At the residence of the intendant, James Hamilton was preparing for racial war, despite the outward insistence that nothing untoward was expected. At his residence, Denmark Vesey was urgently advancing his plans for a night of revolt, despite an outward appearance of docility and obedience. At this same time, a house servant, a free black, and a mulatto—Peter Prioleau, William Pencil, and George Wilson—were each engaged in his own personal drama of treachery and self-survival. And two nights later, on Sunday, June 16, Denmark Vesey's plans were revealed to be fully betrayed.

THE WHITE CHILDREN of Charleston always remembered the night of June 16, 1822. Even those who lived until the early twentieth century, who had survived the artillery bombardment of their city during the Civil War and the murderous racial riots of Reconstruction, could vividly recall in their old age that long-ago Sunday night: when all the white adults appeared unaccustomedly frightened; when there were whispered stories of cruel black men who would slit the throats of white children; when entire families of whites stood outside their houses all night for fear of arson; and when even the smallest children were kept awake until dawn the following day.

For the previous two nights and day prior to that Sunday, Vesey had been able to observe the worried traffic of military couriers and the ominous accumulation of troops and hussars on Charleston's streets. So, too, had the white population. Despite any official pronouncements from the city or state governments, white residents had begun to say among themselves that "something serious was about to take place" among the black population, with rumors centering upon a slave attempt to burn the city and kill all the whites on Sunday night. Although the whites obviously had learned something of the plot, Vesey probably felt confident, secure in the knowledge that at that moment Jesse Blackwood was spreading the call among rural blacks, telling them to come into town prepared to fight the night of June 16.

"I shall never forget the feeling of alarm and anxiety that pervaded the whole community from the time the danger became known, until all risk appeared to be over." So wrote William Hasell Wilson, who was a ten-year-old boy in 1822 and who lived until 1902 to write of Vesey's revolt in his memoirs. Wilson's father was Major John Wilson, the same white master who had sent the family's mulatto slave into the black church to ferret out any talk of revolt. William Wilson recalled that as a boy he had seen this slave frequently in the days before Vesey's revolt "holding mysterious conferences with my father."

On the Sunday evening the revolt was expected, "no one, not even the children, ventured to retire," Wilson later wrote. "The passing of the patrols on the streets, and every slight noise, excited alarm." Intendant Hamilton, who later wrote his own description of the night, perhaps inadvertently also revealed a true verbal picture of the terror among the white population of Charleston. Although commending his militia and the city watch for their steadiness, Hamilton noted that such deportment was all the more remarkable "in a populous town, the streets filled until a late hour with persons, uncertain whether it was safe to *rest* or *not*. . . ."

But the dawn of June 17, Monday, arrived at last, with no clouds of black smoke rising from burning houses, and no cries of whites being murdered by their slaves. "There was a general feeling of relief," William Wilson recalled, at the whites' realization that they had survived the night unharmed. The young Wilson was probably among the hundreds of other white people returning to their homes after their vigil. While they exhaustedly slept, the sun rose higher over Charleston Harbor to the city's east, as if God's blessing were on this Carolina slave city, unmolested after two centuries.

But the deliverance of Charleston was the consequence not of divine intervention but of a secret meeting Sunday afternoon at Vesey's house. Vesey had awakened that morning to the sight of patrols of heavily armed horsemen sloughing their way down Charleston's unpaved sandy streets and a reinforced guard stationed at the State Arsenal. By four o'clock that afternoon, he was meeting at his house with Peter Poyas, Bacchus Hammett, Gullah Jack, and other subordinates to decide whether to go ahead with the attack that midnight. Rolla Bennett later told his judges that "there was a sort of disagreement at Vesey's place," and he may have been referring to a dispute that afternoon between Vesey and his followers over risking all and attacking the city despite the whites' obvious knowledge of the plot. Vesey probably argued the necessity of keeping to the midnight plan. He knew that fifty slaves had arrived that morning by canoe near the city's market. They were either from among the coastal blacks or the French Negroes, armed as best as they were able, and trusting in either Gullah Jack's talismans or Denmark Vesey's generalship to make them free men.

The deciding factor was the appearance at the house that same Sunday afternoon of Jesse Blackwood, the courier Vesey had sent into the countryside. Blackwood reported failure. He had tried twice to travel beyond the city limits, he told Vesey, but each time "the guard was so strict I could not pass them without being taken up." Blackwood may have been lying. (He subsequently testified to his judges, possibly to obtain mercy, that "in fact I had not started and only told him [Vesey] to deceive him.") But it was now clear to Vesey that, whether through black duplicity or white intimidation, the majority of slaves in the Charleston District would not rise up in revolt on June 16.

Vesey acted decisively. On hearing of Blackwood's failure, he sent word to the rural slaves already arrived in Charleston "to depart from the city as soon as possible, and wait for further orders." Gullah Jack was dispatched that same afternoon to tell his recruits at Charleston Neck that "they could not break out that night as the patrol was too strong." The Angolan magician promised the slaves "he would let them know when they were ready." Vesey himself probably still had hopes of eluding the authorities and raising a revolt in the next few days—but he advised Poyas and Gell to burn their lists of recruits, and he began to do the same.

No notices were published in the Monday or Tuesday issues of the Charleston daily newspaper describing the city's extraordinary night of terror. Officially, both the Magnolia Curtain and the Sable Curtain remained intact. But behind those curtains, unofficially reported, the arrests began that week. On the basis either of confessions extracted by cowhide or of information provided by the black spies the canny Hamilton had sent to follow Poyas and Harth, twelve blacks or mulattoes suspected of conspiring in the revolt were now taken into custody.

Peter Poyas, Ned Bennett, and Rolla Bennett were apprehended on June 18; Mingo Harth, on June 21. Remarkably, however, Denmark Vesey himself was not yet detained or even considered a suspect. Vesey certainly knew that, whatever the physical courage of Poyas or the Bennetts, his own name inevitably would be extracted under torture from those and other prisoners at the Work House; but, as the white interrogators and judges later conceded, when Vesey's name was revealed to them that week as the plot's chief organizer, the interrogators' reaction was that he "enjoyed so much the confidence of the whites, that when he was accused, the charge was not only discredited, but he was not even arrested for several days after, and not until the proof of his guilt had become too strong to be doubted."

But what was unthinkable to the white population was apparently common knowledge among Charleston blacks throughout this week. During the later trials, one slave expressed wonderment to his judges that they had not suspected Vesey from the beginning; when Poyas and the Bennetts were taken into custody on June 18, this slave now told his masters after the fact, he had heard "everyone, even the women," in the black community wonder why the whites could be so obtuse as to not also arrest Vesey. Although torn, apparently the social pretense of the Magnolia Curtain and the Sable Curtain was still in part intact, with the whites not yet believing that a free black man treated kindly would revolt, and the blacks for their part saying nothing.

Vesey knew, however, the pretense could not last for long, and perhaps as early as June 17, he left his Bull Street house and went into hiding at the residence of one of his wives in the city. It is possible that he hoped to elude capture and to escape Charleston by stowing away on a ship bound for the Caribbean or the northern states. But by Saturday, June 22, the interrogators at the Work House had heard Vesey's name so frequently that two agents were ordered to arrest him.

His pursuers were an inappropriately named Captain Dove, the commanding officer of the city guard, who had no compunctions about shooting blacks, and Frederick Wesner, a local building contractor who hoped by virtue of Vesey's capture to win political appointment as chief warden of the Work House. As they searched through Charleston's narrow and darkened streets that Saturday night, "a perfect tempest," in their later description, blew in from the ocean; and in the middle of this late-night tropical storm, Dove broke into the house of Vesey's wife and physically seized Denmark Vesey.

Vesey was now in custody at the Work House. The authorities of Charleston were in a hanging mood, and within the next week the trials of Denmark Vesey and his coconspirators began.

CHAPTER SIX

———◈———

The Trials of Vesey and His Conspirators

You have realized the fable of the Frozen Serpent, and attempted to destroy the bosom that sheltered and protected you.
—*Vesey's judges, on pronouncing the sentence of death, 1822*

"DIE LIKE A MAN!" From their common cell at the Work House, Peter Poyas and Denmark Vesey shouted this encouragement to each of the other blacks arrested and brought to the prison during the period from June 18 to June 30. Vesey's and Poyas's shouts gave voice to the fears and anticipations of each black man thrust, under guard, into the city's prison for the confinement and torture of slaves: that once arrested and charged with insurrection, a black slave's death was inevitable, and that a fair trial by whites was an impossibility. The only way to resist was to die stoically and silently, revealing as little about Vesey's plot as possible.

The white authorities at Charleston had a different conception of the imprisonment and trial of blacks. On June 18 James Hamilton, acting on his own initiative after Poyas and nine other blacks were arrested, summoned seven locally prominent merchants and lawyers to convene at twelve noon the following day. Hamilton authorized this group to act as the city's pro tempore court for all blacks arrested that summer for insurrection, and by

June 22, when Denmark Vesey was taken at his wife's house, the court had established its rules and procedures.

No juries were to be impaneled by this special court, and its decisions, including sentences of death, were not appealable to any higher state court. The seven judges were both to hear the cases and to prosecute them. Hamilton later smoothly justified his action in establishing this court by publicly referring to "a statute of a peculiar and local character, and intended for the government of a distinct class of persons"—that is, the Negro Act of 1740, passed by a Barbadian colonial legislature after Hugh Bryan's prophecies and the Stono Rebellion of 1739, and, after two revisions, still in effect in South Carolina in 1822. The act was designed to deal forcefully with any planned or actual slave insurrections, and it authorized the use of special courts for blacks, "severe" physical interrogations, and capital punishment.

Before his execution, Vesey complained bitterly that he "had not had a fair trial, [and] that his accusers had not been brought before him." But the seven magistrates and freeholders sitting on Hamilton's special court were determined to act scrupulously toward the defendants, or at least with as many legal scruples as white Charlestonians might possibly be willing to see applied to blacks in 1822. After first convening, and before hearing any cases of insurrection, Vesey's prosecutor-judges conceded among themselves that they were obligated by the terms of the Negro Act to "depart in many essential features from the principles of common law" in conducting their court. Nevertheless, they decided to offer the defendants such common-law protections as "were not repugnant to" a civilized society. These included the rights to counsel, to know the identities of hostile witnesses, and to cross-examine and challenge as hearsay other slaves' testimonies.

A social system that both enslaved human beings and sought to provide the enslaved with legal counsel did not necessarily appear illogical or contradictory to white Charlestonians of the 1820s. The court was simply another aspect of a highly compartmentalized social compact imposed upon blacks: The slave existed as both a person and a nonperson, both an I-Thou and an I-It. Nor were the city judges necessarily opening their court to legal debate by appointing these counsels of record, many of whom were not attorneys. In the cases of defendants who were slaves, the counsels recognized by the court usually were the slaves' owners. (Hence, the judges' allowance of counsel may have been an act not of benevolence toward blacks but of self-protection against later legal actions. If a slave was found guilty and executed, the slave's owner, having been present at the trial and encouraged to examine the evidence, could not protest that he had been denied the use of his property without due process.) One attorney, Jacob Axon, who at their owners' requests did represent several slaves who were not his property, later accepted appointment as a presiding judge in the Vesey conspiracy when one of the original freeholders became ill. Denmark Vesey's own counsel, as will be seen, also possessed questionable loyalty to his client.

Other existing court records support Vesey's charge against his judges that they tried his case contrary to the principles of common law they had promised, at least in part, to uphold. The most censorious public comment against this court, however, did not come from Vesey or any other black defendant. (Their cries and opinions, after all, would not have been heard outside their prison cells.) It came, surprisingly, from a white aristocrat of the same social and economic class as James Hamilton and the city's judges.

Two days after Intendant Hamilton convened his special court, and even before any news of the trials had appeared in print, a remarkable article was submitted for anonymous publication in the *Charleston Courier* for June 21. Entitled "Melancholy Effect of Popular Excitement," this article purported to be nothing more than "a simple narrative of facts" concerning events in South Carolina more than a decade earlier. Recalling an incident "within the recollections of thousands," the unidentified author recounted how at that time a drunken militia member had one night sounded the alarm for an attack, provoking white residents to fear an immediate revolt by slaves. An innocent slave named Billy was seized as the "ringleader" simply because he possessed an antiquated trumpet allegedly capable of calling his fellow slaves to arms, though the instrument in Billy's cabin was "covered and even filled with cobwebs." A local magistrate ordered Billy to be hanged. Both the slave's owner and a certain "judicial character" protested against what these two white men termed a "legal murder." But so excited was the local populace—and so politically ambitious was the magistrate who ordered the hanging of the unfortunate Billy—"that it is not certain that a pardon could have saved him."

Within the small society of aristocratic white residents at Charleston, the author of "Melancholy Effect" was widely known to be William Johnson, an associate justice of the U.S. Supreme Court and the husband of Governor William Bennett's sister. Concealed within this seemingly innocuous article was an implied criticism of Intendant Hamilton, a political competitor to the governor. Bennett and his brother-in-law were both of the opinion that Hamilton had exaggerated the seriousness of the rumored slave revolt, and that he had misused the authority of his office in arranging this special court for the trial of Vesey and the other defendants, who included three slaves from the governor's own household. Hence, for Charleston's *cognoscenti*, this casually submitted anecdote in a local newspaper was, in fact, a pointed political allegory. Bennett and Johnson could be interpreted, respectively, as the aggrieved slave owner and the "judicial character" who tried to uphold justice and order, while Hamilton and his handpicked judges could be interpreted as the exciters of public hysteria and the executioners of "legal murder."

The judges of the court, who included members of Charleston's foremost white families, understood as well as anyone the social code by which aristocrats of this city insulted one another. Such prominent judges on the court as James Legaré and William Drayton fulminated to themselves the week of June 22–29, while they were hearing the trial, that Justice Johnson had violated "decency and propriety" by suggesting in print that this "Court, under the influence of popular prejudice, was capable of committing perjury and murder." Yet despite this indignation expressed by their judges, Vesey's and Poyas's angry shouts from their prison cell to each defendant—"Die like a man!"—persist in the historical imagination. Justice Johnson's unspoken question continues to hang in the air 177 years later: Did Charleston's special court commit "legal murder" during the last week of June 1822, against Vesey and his fellow defendants?

The answer is yes. In historical fairness to Vesey's judges, it must be emphasized that the establishment of this court was at that time fully legal under the Negro Act; moreover, numerous consistencies in the uncoerced testimonies of slave witnesses in later trials that summer indicate to a reasonable person that Vesey certainly had been planning an insurrection. But during Vesey's trial itself, his judges failed to prove his guilt by the very standards of common-law conduct that they themselves had promised to uphold in their court. Despite their prior agreements that the identities of hostile witnesses be known to the defendants and that "the testimony of one witness, unsupported by additional evidence, or circumstances, should lead to no conviction of a *capital* nature," the judges made an exception in the case of Denmark Vesey.

Of the four slave testimonies against Vesey in the court records (there were no witnesses recorded for his defense), only one witness, Frank Ferguson, testified specifically that Vesey had urged the city's slaves to seize weapons from the white population and fight for their freedom. The other three, including an anonymous "Witness No. 1," testified only in general terms, impugning Vesey's character before his judges, but hardly corroborating Ferguson's testimony. Vesey, they claimed, "would not like to have a white man in his presence" and "was bitter toward the whites." The sole white witness against Vesey, an adolescent male who frequently overheard the defendant talking in his workplace, could tell the judges only about Vesey's "general conversation," which the boy said usually "was about religion . . . as, for instance, [Vesey] would speak of the creation of the world, in which he would say all men had equal rights, blacks as well as whites—all his religious remarks were mingled with slavery."

The physical evidence available to the judges also was notably scanty for the requirements of arrest and prosecution, and much less so for the imposition of a sentence of death. None of the lists of slave rebels, numbering in the thousands, that Vesey and his lieutenants were said to have kept was introduced into evidence; nor were these lists ever located by the white authorities. The pikes and spears that Gullah Jack had carried into the country had not yet been discovered by the plantation owners there, and these weapons also were not offered as evidence or even mentioned by the judges during Vesey's trial. A handful of weapons did eventually turn up after Vesey's conviction, and the judges almost certainly were correct in guessing that Vesey and his lieutenants had secretly burned their lists of recruits on or about June 16, before their arrests; but as any competent defense counsel could have pointed out, this evidence was moot, and merely speculative whether or not Vesey was guilty.

There was one item of supposedly hard evidence. Intendant Hamilton, aided by Captain Dove and Frederick Wesner of the city guard, claimed to have located the unidentified white barber whom they said Vesey had deceived into making wigs of Caucasian hair for the black rebels to wear on the night of the revolt. Hamilton personally brought this hairdresser into Vesey's cell and asked the prisoner if he knew him. When Vesey stated that he did not, Hamilton suddenly drew out of his pocket such a wig and made his accusation. "Good God!" his captors recorded Vesey as exclaiming, and then, according to their court narrative, after remaining silent a moment or two, the prisoner confessed that he did know the man and that the wig had been made for his own use.

On such slender evidence and testimony was Vesey's fate determined. Particularly troublesome to historians has been the lack of weapons produced as evidence during Vesey's trial or those of his conspirators. Of the "hundreds" of pikes, guns, and daggers about which numerous slaves testified later that Vesey had arranged to have them cached throughout the city for use on the night of the revolt, the prosecution was able eventually to present only six pike poles (not yet fitted with blades), less than a dozen hammered daggers or swords, and a keg of musket balls discovered accidentally underneath a wharf. The judges apparently concluded, as have many historians since, that Vesey simply had exaggerated the number of weapons available to his recruits, hoping that, once committed, they would continue fighting even if inadequately armed. Like all revolutionaries, Vesey believed that a well-armed cadre, not a fully equipped people's army, precipitated revolt. "Let us assemble a sufficient number to commence work with spirit," Vesey often told his earliest recruiters, "and we'll not want men. They'll fall in behind us fast enough." But the legal irregularities of Vesey's trial and the lack of evidence convinced one white historian more than a century later that the Vesey plot never in fact existed.

Writing in 1964, Richard C. Wade asserted that in the summer of 1822, "Charleston stumbled into tragedy. The 'plot' was probably never more than loose talk by aggrieved and bitter men." In addition to the paucity of weapons available to the potential recruits, Wade also noted that Denmark Vesey was "the only free Negro executed" consequent to the city's trials. By this argument, Vesey was singled out for nineteenth-century prosecution, and twentieth-century celebration, only because of his civil and economic uniqueness. Wade's position is not necessarily revisionist. A later generation of scholars can frame his argument within the emergent categories of political correctness and incorrectness. The civic white authorities of nineteenth-century Charleston *needed* the conviction and execution of Denmark Vesey, according to Wade's argument, in order to demonstrate that economically "pampered" blacks would inevitably betray the white social order; conversely, twentieth-century black historians needed the life and death of Denmark Vesey as a convenient emblem, in Wade's words, of "the latent urge for freedom that lay beneath the regime of bondage."

Wade's categorical finding that the Vesey plot never existed was disproved in part by both white and black historians of the 1960s and 1970s, who demonstrated that Wade had, inadvertently, misidentified some manuscript confessions by the conspirators and discounted any threat by armed slaves. Yet, his interpretation is not wholly disproved. If we set aside for the moment questions of common law and rules of evidence, an economic and demographic agenda also was undeniably working against Denmark Vesey during his trial.

Since the colonial era, police action against blacks in South Carolina had frequently been determined by the state of the economy. Economic panics had been followed by rumors of slave revolts in 1700, 1720, and again in 1740, when Hugh Bryan had begun his apocalyptic prophecies. By the nineteenth century, the economy of South Carolina had become based on one crop, and there appears a correlation between the market value of the state's exported short-staple cotton, particularly in the important English market, and the black revolts that white low-country planters feared at home. In 1816, for example, the value of Charleston cotton varied per pound by a significant four cents; that same year, an incipient slave revolt was rumored but never proved among the burgeoning black population at the low-country town of

Camden. (The correlation between cotton's market value and rumored slave revolts may also have been affected by the slave owners' tendency to sell slaves regardless of family ties, to reduce rations, or to increase the gang-labor quotas whenever the prices of cotton dropped.)

Similarly, during June and July of 1822—when Denmark Vesey was on trial for his life—the value of South Carolina's exported cotton varied by four to seven cents per pound, the greatest market uncertainty since 1815. As a restorative to social order, the white authorities may have started their usual search for a black scapegoat, and Vesey and his companions may have ascended a gallows because at the port of Liverpool the price of Charleston cotton that month had plunged a few cents.

But such theorizing more than a century after the fact denies to Denmark Vesey what his Charleston judges historically were unwilling to acknowledge in him: his capacity to act as a free individual, and his courage in confronting the military and economic forces against him. Vesey's circumstances during his imprisonment and trial should not be forgotten: "By a vote of the court, all spectators were excluded," a contemporary source recorded, "except the owners and counsel of the slaves concerned. No other colored person was allowed to enter the jail, and a strong guard of soldiers was kept always on duty around the building." Nor should the Work House's recorded use of the black hole and cowhide against intransigent prisoners be forgotten.

All the more remarkable, then, was Vesey's stamina and courage in insisting that he personally be allowed in the Work House courtroom to cross-examine the black and mulatto witnesses brought against him. "He at first questioned them [the witnesses] in the dictatorial, despotic manner in which he was probably accustomed to address them," his judges later wrote. "But this not producing the desired effect, he questioned them with affected surprise and concern for learning false testimony against him; still failing in his purpose, he then examined them strictly as to dates, but could not make them contradict themselves."

Such, at least, is the version supplied by Vesey's judges, and no text of his actual cross-examination was recorded by the court. But there was also another cross-examiner present at the Work House courtroom: a white attorney, possibly selected to represent Vesey through the influence of Captain Joseph Vesey. Colonel George Warren Cross had been accepted by the court as Vesey's attorney of record; he was the son of Captain George Cross, with whom Captain Vesey had done business at Charleston since the 1790s. It is possible that Captain Vesey, then in his seventies, roused himself from his retirement in order to arrange a legal defense for his former slave; but this same Colonel Cross also had been among the militia commanders ordered to patrol the city's streets on the night of Vesey's revolt. The presence of this counsel, whose motivations were apparently divided, may have been another attempt to seal an already certain conviction for slave insurrection.

Regardless of the character of his defense, Denmark Vesey seemed sure of the trial's conclusion as the legal examinations of the defendants neared a close during the last week of June. From their shared cell, Vesey and Poyas kept up their shouts to their fellow black prisoners of the only option available to them when the court announced its verdict: die like men.

ON THURSDAY, June 27, Vesey was brought into the small upstairs room at the Work House to hear the verdict of the court. Seated before him were the seven judges, as well as Intendant Hamilton, whom Vesey had hoped to see assassinated. Vesey now was seated, his legs manacled.

"Denmark Vesey," the presiding justice, Lionel H. Kennedy, read, "the court on mature consideration, has pronounced you guilty." The verdict meant death.

The justice continued, probably emphasizing with his voice the words he later chose to italicize in his published text. "It is difficult to imagine what *infatuation* could have prompted you to attempt an enterprise so wild and visionary. You were a free man; you were comparatively wealthy; and enjoyed every comfort compatible with your situation. You had, therefore, much to risk, and little to gain. From your age and experience, you *ought* to have known that success was impractible."

There was more. Now employing a classical allusion, Justice Kennedy continued: "Reared by the hand of kindness, and fostered by a master who assumed many of the duties of a parent— you have realized the fable of the Frozen Serpent, and attempted to destroy the bosom that sheltered and protected you." The justice then recalled the biblical example of the thief repentant at Calvary. "You cannot have forgotten the history of the malefactor on the Cross, who, like yourself, was the wretched and deluded victim of offended justice. His conscience was awakened in the pangs of dissolution, and yet there is reason to believe that his spirit was received into the realms of bliss. May *you* imitate his example, and may *your* last moments prove like his!"

In order that his life and actions not be publicly commemorated, any black person, man or woman, seen wearing mourning in the streets of Charleston within a week of his execution was to be arrested and whipped.

Neither at his sentencing nor at his hanging did Denmark Vesey speak. But as he listened to these words, seated in his habitual posture with arms crossed over his chest but with his eyes fixed upon some remote spot on the courtroom floor perceivable only to him, his judges saw, or later wrote in their report that they saw, tears on Denmark Vesey's face.

It may never have happened. The tears may have been just a

sententious detail fictionally added by his judges to a publication by which they hoped to paint a moral example. Suspiciously, it is the only passage in their official account in which there is even a partial description of his face.

Or Denmark Vesey may indeed have cried—cried for private reasons of grief, fear, remorse, or outrage. The reason why he may have wept upon hearing the sentence of death in that small, heavily guarded room at Charleston will remain unknown.

But if, in fact, during the last week of his life Denmark Vesey silently wept, his tears had been a long time coming.

CHAPTER SEVEN

The Shock of Executions:
Denmark Vesey as a National Figure

Twenty-two human beings, black, were executed at Charleston on the morning of the 26th ult.
—New York Daily Advertiser, *August 5, 1822*

There can be no harm in the salutary inculcation of one lesson, among a certain *portion of our population, that there is nothing they are bad enough to do, that we are not powerful enough to punish.*
—*Charleston Intendant James Hamilton, August 16, 1822*

"AH! SLAVERY IS A *hard* business, and I am afraid that in this country we shall know it to our bitter cost some day or other." So wrote Mrs. Mary Lamboll Beach of Charleston in a letter dated July 5, 1822, to her sister in Philadelphia. Mrs. Beach, a middle-aged widow, wrote to assure her sister and other northern relatives that despite fears three days earlier of a slave uprising to prevent Denmark Vesey's execution, she and the other white inhabitants of the city were safe. "I believe *all* dangers for the *present* season are over—but to any one at all disposed to reflect, or feel for *others* as well as their own interests, the events of this week were calculated to excite *much painful* and *bitter* reflection. The execution is over, as to us, at least for the present, and has not been attended with insult, or assistance, as was feared by some of weak nerves."

This last comment indicates that even a pious widow found it necessary to maintain a brave front toward Charleston's black population on the day Denmark Vesey was hanged. Yet, in her subsequent fifteen letters to her Philadelphia relations that summer, Mary Beach reveals herself as a remarkably informed and sensitive observer of the Vesey executions. Her letters contain reliable information on matters on which the Charleston newspapers officially had maintained a near-silence since the Vesey affair had begun. The *Courier*, for example, despite the presence of five hundred armed militiamen in the city, confined its notice of Vesey's execution on July 2 to only a few lines of small type. The newspaper noted that "DENMARK VESEY (a free black man)," along with Rolla Bennett, Batteau Bennett, Ned Bennett, Peter Poyas, and Jesse Blackwood, had been hanged that morning between 6:00 and 8:00 a.m. upon conviction "of attempt to raise an insurrection in this State." (The item immediately following this notice in the newspaper, on the election of officers of the Charleston Bible Society, was twice as long.)

Through the Beach correspondence, events of the last days of Vesey's life can be historically revisited, albeit from a white religious perspective. Mary Beach was an active member of the Independent Congregational Circular Church, a "liberal" white denomination within the city, and members of this church undertook to visit Vesey and Peter Poyas in their cell. These missionary visits did not go well. "When interrogated to what church he belonged," Beach later wrote her sister, Vesey replied "with a very firm descriptive tone, 'None'." His visitors found Vesey "in a very hardened state," and the churchmen reported that "Vesey and Poyas' fellow would hear nothing they had to say; [Vesey and Poyas] said they were condemned already, and it was no use to say anything more." Peter Poyas, Beach wrote, "was particularly observed to be a villain."

This estimation of Poyas was shared by his judges, although a later century's interpretation of his character would differ. Poyas, a "first-rate" ship's carpenter, had been a steadfast advocate of the revolt during the conspiracy, and together with Vesey had withstood the rigors of their imprisonment. When the sentence of death was announced, Poyas's only response—"and that not in a very supplicating tone," his judges later observed—had been to comment, "I suppose you'll let me see my wife and family before I die?"

As the date of the July 2 executions neared, "the Negroes were under the impression that Denmark Vesey, the freed black, *would* be delivered, if in no other way the jail door opened by a supernatural power," Beach wrote. This belief may have been sustained by the city's diaspora of A.M.E. blacks, who recalled from the New Testament the miraculous deliverance of the apostles Paul and Silas from the Roman jail at Philippi. Or perhaps it had its origins in an entirely different religion. "Gullah Jack" Pritchard, the Obeah-man whom Vesey had recruited, was not yet arrested, and until the morning of July 2, he tried unsuccessfully to rouse the district's Angolan and Ibo slaves through rituals to arm themselves and attempt a desperate rescue of Vesey. (After his detention, and prior to his execution, Gullah Jack told his captors that what he feared most at the gallows was meeting with the wraith of Denmark Vesey, angry because in life he had not been rescued.)

But on the night before Vesey's execution, the religious reassurances that he and Poyas had refused to discuss with their white visitors were apparently openly expressed among the black prisoners in their cells. "I heard that Vesey said in jail that it was a glorious cause he was to die for," Mary Beach later wrote her sister, "and the singing of Psalms in there the night before was carried on to a *great* extent." Shortly before sunrise on July 2, the first six condemned to be hanged—Vesey, Poyas, the three Bennetts, and Jesse Blackwood—were herded outside the Work House to be taken to their deaths. "I am told two of them even laughed when first brought out of the jail, and preserved this state of mind even to the last," Beach wrote.

Vesey and the five others, according to Hamilton's later statement, were taken to be hanged at an unspecified site at Blake's Lands. This was a desolate expanse of about 152 acres north of the city's limits and well beyond Charleston's usual choice of location for the execution of pirates and other white criminals. Even in the mid-twentieth century, when the city had expanded as a major military port, Blake's Lands was an underpopulated area shunned by Charlestonians, both black and white. Writing in 1943, John Bennett, a descendant of Governor Thomas Bennett, described Blake's Lands as "a wild, unkempt savannah of broomsedge grass and undrained tidal marsh. . . . Into this savannah creeps a lagoon, at high tide filled with salt water; but at other times only a tangled stretch of marsh grass and mire. At its edge stood a little patch of oak woods." Blake's Lands, despite the tedious journey there for the hangman and the guards, probably was chosen as Vesey's execution site by the city because its remoteness as a killing field made less likely any demonstration by the city's blacks on the day of execution, or its later commemoration as the site of Vesey's martyrdom. The trapdoor gallows of the later nineteenth century was not then in common use, and it is likely that the stand of oak trees, the only noticeable feature in this otherwise-marshy landscape, was the means of execution. If Vesey or any of his companions spoke before they were hanged, the words were not recorded by authorities. Apparently keeping the promise made to one another in their jail cells, Vesey and his companions died in silence.

Despite the city's efforts to keep the executions secret, there were, according to a contemporary observer, "immense crowds of blacks and whites . . . present at the scene." True to the court's promise to Vesey, the city promulgated an ordinance that any black person publicly seen wearing mourning clothes after the July 2 executions would be arrested and flogged. Remarkably, some blacks defied this ordinance. A free black who was a contemporary to Vesey would tell Union officers later in the nineteenth century that "several" slaves were "abused in the street, and some put into prison, for wearing sackcloth. . . . They generally got the law, which is thirty nine lashes."

Also true to its word, the court and city authorities publicly refused to disclose the final disposition of Vesey's body. For over a century and a half, Denmark Vesey's final gravesite was unknown. Even the location of his execution became a subject of dispute. From the 1820s onward, some black residents insisted that Vesey was not executed with his other conspirators at Blake's Lands as was first stated by Hamilton. Instead, they maintained, in an actively oral tradition, that Vesey had been hanged from a large live oak tree along the city's Ashley Avenue. There may be truth in this oral tradition. Ashley Avenue is much closer to the site of the Work House, and it was conveniently near the city's Potter's Field cemetery, which would have allowed for a quick and anonymous burial that same night. Intendant Hamilton certainly was capable of the stratagem of deliberately misidentifying Vesey's execution site, and the blacks' story gained acceptance among the white population. In 1954, the *A.M.E. Church Review*, the national bulletin of that predominantly black denomination, featured a description of the "Denmark Vesey oak tree" on its inside front cover. Well into the late twentieth century, some white residents of Charleston would proudly point out to northern visitors the "Ashley Avenue Oak" as the tree from which the black rebel Denmark Vesey had been hanged.

EVEN AFTER VESEY'S DEATH, the racial violence and executions continued throughout the summer of 1822. Within two weeks of Vesey's hanging, three slaves were sentenced to death for having fired shots at the Charleston mail coach as it passed through the suburb of Parker's Ferry. (Parker's Ferry was the settlement where Vesey and other blacks may have talked with the Islamic slave and teacher Omar Ibn Said.) Within the city of Charleston, Hamilton and his seven judges intensified their civic prosecutions and executions of blacks. By the end of four weeks after Vesey's hanging, the court had ordered the arrests of 73 additional blacks on charges of having participated in his conspiracy. Included in this number were Vesey's surviving lieutenants Gullah Jack and Bacchus Hammett. By the end of August, when the city court adjourned, a total of 131 blacks had been arrested; 35 had been sent to their deaths.

By the middle of July, Vesey and all those identified as his chief coconspirators were dead and no longer a threat to Charleston. It is evident, however, that Hamilton kept the court in session for an additional month in order to conduct an official campaign of terror against Charleston's black population in general and the remnants of the A.M.E. congregation in particular. Vesey's firm answer of "None" when questioned on his church membership may have been an attempt to shield what was left of the A.M.E. church, or to conceal how he had used its ecclesiastical organization to recruit a band of revolutionaries. This ruse had worked for a while. Throughout his trial and his subsequent sentencing, there was no recorded discussion by his judges of Vesey's membership in the church, or his position as a class leader in that denomination.

But after Vesey's execution on July 2, fourteen of the blacks arrested that month were specifically identified by Hamilton and the court as former A.M.E. members. Some of those arrested, as well as those already incarcerated at the Work House, told Hamilton and the court what they wanted to hear. *"All the African Church was engaged in it,"* William Paul, the slave, emphatically testified to his judges. Other black prisoners, despite the possibility of torture or death, were adamant in protecting the church, or at least the free black who was its local organizer, the Reverend Morris Brown. Monday Gell, one of Vesey's original coconspirators, in a rare show of courage testified to the court that "Morris Brown knew nothing of it, and we [Vesey and Gell] agreed not to let him [know]." Hamilton may have wished the further prosecution of Morris Brown, but, with such inconclusive testimonies, he had to content himself with a legal order expelling Brown permanently from the state.

The intendant took pains, however, to inform Charleston's white population about the evils of Vesey's former place of worship. "Among the conspirators, a *majority* of them belonged to the *African Church*," Hamilton announced to the city on August 16. (Actually, the number was a plurality.) He characterized the A.M.E. congregation as a "hotbed" of Vesey's revolutionary ideas, "in which the germ might well be expected to spring into life and vigor." Hamilton omitted any mention whatever of Vesey's membership in the largely white congregation of the Second Presbyterian Church, which through mid-1822 was recorded on the presbytery rolls and was accessible to the city authorities. The larger agenda of publicly identifying black congregations with potential slave revolts was obviously the intention of Hamilton and the city judges; and that Denmark Vesey also had worshipped at an established white church under the supervision of a white minister was disregarded as an inconvenient fact. By the end of the month, what remained of the A.M.E.'s church building had been burned to the ground, on the city's orders.

On July 12, two more convicted conspirators, "Gullah Jack" Pritchard and John Horry, were hanged at The Lines, an area of abandoned earthworks marking the city's northern limits. This area was much more accessible to spectators than Blake's Lands. On July 26, a large crowd gathered along Meeting Street to watch twenty-two additional conspirators taken under guard to be hanged that morning at The Lines.

The extraordinary number of condemned prisoners, and the dispatch with which the city authorities hoped to execute them in one day, almost certainly was intended by the Charleston government as a showcase of its police response to the Vesey plot. Unlike the covert executions and burials of Vesey and his five chief coconspirators on July 2, these executions had been advertised several days in advance in the *Courier*, and, on the morning of July 26, each of the twenty-two condemned slaves was paraded, riding in a cart atop his own coffin, in a procession toward The Lines. Doubtless the city government thought this spectacle would intimidate blacks with the thoroughness of its prosecution, and impress whites with its reimposition of public order. In the presentation of mass executions as a political pageantry, however, the city government failed in its performance of the details.

Police states, of which antebellum Charleston was an early model, fail surprisingly often in their attention to detail, an activity where totalitarianism by definition should be expected to excel. In the twentieth century, for instance, concentration camp guards, because they are allowed to do anything, sometimes get drunk and fail to murder *all* the prisoners; or the introduction of mimeographic machinery into a closed society to facilitate state orders also makes possible a samizdat literature of individual freedom. On that Friday morning in 1822 reserved for mass executions, Intendant Hamilton and the city judges also botched their institutional show of force because of a lack of attention to the details of crowd control, and an inept hangman.

Although an "immense crowd" of blacks and whites, in Mary Beach's description, had been encouraged to gather along Meeting Street and The Lines to witness the executions ("not with ladies, understand"), no one in authority apparently had thought about the danger of hundreds of carriages, horsemen, and pedestrians excitedly pressed closely together. Consequently, when "a horse started," and "the troops immediately made a move to clear the ground," in Beach's description, "you may form some idea of *such a crowd falling* back." A young black coachman of a prominent white family was knocked from the family's vehicle and fatally run over; and "several persons were hurt," presumably white as well as black, in the general pushing, stumbling, and falling.

When order was at last restored, and the twenty-two condemned slaves were shepherded toward a temporary scaffolding to be hanged from three wooden cross beams, it was discovered that the hangman had botched his preparations. "Owing to some bad arrangement in preparing the ropes," an anonymous "Colored American" historian later reported to the northern press, the condemned after their falls from the scaffold neither had their necks quickly snapped nor lapsed into unconsciousness—"they, in their agony of strangulation, begged earnestly to be dispatched; which was done by pistol shot by the Captain of the City Guard, who was always prepared for such an emergency: *i.e., shooting slaves.*"

Rather than impressing the whites and striking awe among the blacks, the July 26 executions were a horrific mess. Nevertheless, the city of Charleston persevered. Four more black prisoners were hanged at The Lines on July 30. The thirty-fifth condemned slave, William Garner, was hanged there on August 9. Vesey's execution and those of his convicted conspirators were like an exacerbated sore on the surface of Charleston that would not heal.

U.S. Supreme Court Justice William Johnson, who had been the first public critic of the city's actions, was appalled by the executions and conduct of Intendant Hamilton and the court. "I have now passed my half-century, and begun to feel lonely among the men of the present day," Justice Johnson wrote to his friend, the retired President Thomas Jefferson. "I have lived to see what I really never believed it possible I should see—courts held with closed doors, and men dying by the scores who had never seen the faces nor heard the voices of their accusers."

Other white Charlestonians also were becoming uneasy, but from more pecuniary motives. In that economically depressed year of 1822, there could be little profit to a Charleston planter in selling his slaves if a potential buyer feared his new property might be seized by Hamilton's court. On July 16, the Charleston financial agent John Potter wrote to his northern friend Langdon Cheves, a director of the United States Bank, detailing the value of Cheves's stock certificates and other southern holdings: "As for *Negroes,* I do not believe they would bring any price at present."

There were also a few small, still voices within the white community who found the trials and executions reprehensible on religious grounds. Mary Beach was privately horrified to hear rumors that domestic slaves within her own household were under suspicion by the city's court, and in possible danger of arrest and execution. "Ours as *yet* have not been implicated," she later wrote her sister on July 23, "but this is no security that some of them may not perish on the gallows in ten days; if it should be the case, I fear I should be a wretched being to the end of my days for having held them in a state of slavery to prove a temptation." That "young man, Hamilton, our Intendant," she wrote her sister, "knows not God."

By the end of that summer, northerners other than Beach's relatives had read of Vesey's execution and plot, and opinions were being promulgated in more national forums. "White men, too, would engender plots and escape from their imprisonment were they situated as are these miserable children of Africa," editorialized the New York *Daily Advertiser* on July 31. The Hartford, Connecticut, *Courant* noted the curious near-silence on Vesey's execution and attempted insurrection as reported in the Charleston papers but told its readers that letters received from the southern city reported that Vesey's death "has created much alarm, and that two brigades of troops were under arms for some time to suppress any risings that might have taken place." By the last week of August, the Boston *Evening Gazette* had qualifiedly approved Vesey's plot at Charleston: "Strictly speaking, nobody can blame the servile part of the population (the blacks) for attempting to escape from bondage, however their delusions may be regretted." Also by the end of August, after Vesey and thirty-four other blacks had been hanged, the *Daily Advertiser* opined again: "As yet nothing has appeared that has met our view to justify the great sacrifice of human lives that has taken place. . . . Certain it is that neither the spirit nor letter of the law, under which these executions have taken place, sanctions the enormous sacrifice."

Nothing piqued aristocratic Charlestonians so much as a perceived insult to their local pride, particularly in the northern press. By that autumn, two of the presiding magistrates of the city court, Lionel Kennedy and Thomas Parker, authorized and edited a publication at Charleston of what purportedly was a full account of Vesey's trial and sentencing. The title, at least, was fully revealing: *An Official Report of the Trials of Sundry Negroes, Charged with an Attempt to Raise an Insurrection in the State of South Carolina: Preceded by an Introduction and Narrative.* Kennedy and Parker probably hoped to emulate the success of a prior northern publication, *The New York Conspiracy, or a History of the Negro Plot 1741–42*, an account of the slave rebellion in that colony which first had been published in 1810 to a generally receptive white readership. "As a very general desire has been expressed to be informed of the details of the plot," Kennedy and Parker wrote in their introduction, their report undertook to present the "whole evidence" in the trials, sentencing, and executions of Vesey and each of his coconspirators.

Surprisingly, the judges chose in the *Official Report* to preserve a verbal accuracy in the testimonies and cross-examination of the black defendants. "Although a different style might have been more agreeable to the ear," Kennedy and Parker wrote, they made no attempt to change the "phraseology, which was generally in the very words used by the witnesses." This was true as far as it went. Although there are no patronizingly phonetic spellings of black dialect within the report's text, or attempts to render into nineteenth-century English prose the complexities of the Gullah language, Vesey, Poyas, Gullah Jack, and others are recorded speaking in their individual voices on the few occasions they are quoted directly in the *Official Report*. These rare occasions evoke perhaps more emotional response in a reader than the judges intended—for instance, Vesey's simple exclamation of "Good God!" when confronted with a barber's wig and the lengths to which a city police state would go to locate or fabricate evidence of his guilt, or Poyas's stoic response on hearing his sentence of death, "I suppose you'll let me see my wife and family before I die?"

The *Official Report* failed as a document of legal and political justification in the perspectives of both the nineteenth and the twentieth century. Twentieth-century scholars have pointed out that, despite the promise of presenting the "whole evidence," the text of *Official Report* contains few transcripts of defense cross-examinations, no testimonies of friendly witnesses, and no defense arguments by court-appointed attorneys in the cases of Vesey and many other defendants. Upon the report's nineteenth-century publication, Kennedy and Parker's printed boast in their book's conclusion that Vesey and the other condemned in the Charleston trials had merely been hanged, rather than burned alive as blacks had been after the New York trials of 1741, did not score the humanitarian points in the northern press that they had hoped. And many whites in the South, remembering Denmark Vesey's literacy, questioned the wisdom of publishing this document preserving the voices of slave resistance and detailing how closely Charleston had come to its destruction by blacks. In 1841, a northern woman visiting South Carolina, on being told for the first time of Vesey's revolt, asked her hosts if she might see a copy of Kennedy and Parker's official report. According to the account later published in the *Atlantic Monthly*, "she was cautiously told that the only copy in the house, after being carefully kept for years under lock and key, had been burnt at last, lest it should reach the dangerous eyes of slaves. The same thing had happened, it was added, in many families."

The Charleston judges also had been preempted by their city supervisor, Intendant Hamilton. Within six weeks of Vesey's execution, Hamilton had, politically and literarily, ridden the back of black revolt toward his ambition of higher public office. His version of the trials and executions, *Negro Plot: An Account of the Late Intended Insurrection Among a Portion of the Blacks of the City of Charleston, South Carolina*, was published more than a month before the court's report that autumn, first appearing on August 16, 1822. (The last of Vesey's companions had been hanged only seven days earlier.) *Negro Plot* proved to be much more widely circulated than *Official Report*; Hamilton's book went through four editions, including two published in Boston. His account of Vesey's plot does not differ substantially from Kennedy and Parker's report, but the intendant emphasized in his writing the alacrity with which he personally had recognized and defeated "a scheme so wicked and atrocious" as the black revolt. Officially acclaimed as "the hero of Charleston" by the South Carolina legislature after the book's appearance, Hamilton was elected later that year to the U.S. Congress. There he became a national champion of nullification, or the doctrine of states' rights. Within less than a decade, he was elected governor of the state; and, by the mid-1830s, Hamilton was being considered, like his political idol John C. Calhoun, as a potential vice-presidential candidate.

The state legislature's praise of Intendant Hamilton after Vesey's execution was also a tacit rebuke to Governor Thomas Bennett. Angry because of the deaths of three slaves within his household, Bennett had continued to argue with legislators that the extent of the slave conspiracy had been exaggerated and that the primary motivators of black discontent had been only a few freemen, such as Denmark Vesey and black sailors from other ports, unwisely manumitted. In a special message to the legislature on November 28, 1822, Bennett officially reproached the Charleston authorities for their mass executions of the Vesey conspirators. At such spectacles as the twenty-two blacks hanged in one day, Bennett wrote, "humanity wept." He then proceeded to suggest to the legislators an opinion that, less than a generation later, would be unthinkable to any other white southern politician: that black slavery was a moral evil, and was accepted by whites only because of historical or financial expediency. "Slavery abstractly considered would perhaps lead every mind to the same conclusion; but the period has long since passed when a correction might have been applied." Given the inevitability of black slavery, Bennett seems to have suggested that the better course for public men in the South was to adopt a stoic indifference toward such radicals as Denmark Vesey or Intendant Hamilton. "The institution [of slavery] is established," Bennett wrote, in a tone of both finality and resignation. "The evil is entailed."

The political antagonism growing in 1822 between the adherents of Bennett and those of Hamilton strangely began to prefigure the similar schism in southern politics more than four generations later, during the civil rights conflicts of the 1950s and 1960s. Bennett's reactions resembled those of twentieth-century Bourbon southern governors, insistent that their black populations were happy, and that only the presence of "outside agitators" fomented racial strife. By contrast, Hamilton's political career was more akin to a later generation of twentieth-century southern governors, such as the young George C. Wallace, perfectly willing to exploit populist fears of blacks for the sake of personal advancement.

The new men of nineteenth-century South Carolina prevailed. Bennett's unpopularity with the legislature made it impossible for him to seek reelection in 1822; his successor as governor was Major John Wilson, whose mulatto slave, George, had spied voluntarily upon the Vesey conspirators. Bennett's friend and brother-in-law, U.S. Supreme Court Justice William Johnson, also was ostracized politically and socially for having criticized the Vesey trials. Johnson eventually found it necessary to move his family permanently to Philadelphia. By this time, the city of Charleston had issued ordinances restricting the education and religious instruction of slaves, and requiring the temporary imprisonment of any freed black seamen who dared enter the port city. ("If such be the law of this country, this shall not long be my country," Johnson had written to Thomas Jefferson before departing Charleston.)

Denmark Vesey's execution on July 2 had been the final rending in the city's Magnolia and Sable curtains: Whites could no longer act as if they were inviolable and benevolent, and they could no longer assume that their black slaves were subservient and harmless. "I have heard it remarked by several [whites] that *all* confidence in them is now forever at an end," Mary Beach had written on July 5. Beach then described the reaction of a mutual friend in Charleston to the Vesey plot, a Mary Jones, who had stated "in a most solemn tone—'Oh! I shall never be able to bear the sight of a Negro again, and if I go (or live to go to the Northward) I *never will* have *one* about me!'" This friend, Mary Beach wrote, "has almost, I may say, a hatred of them *all*."

Vesey's execution also had two more effects with national consequences. On July 22, Secretary of War Calhoun ordered the transfer of U.S. military forces from Florida to indefinite duty at Charleston. The reason given, as Calhoun stated in his order, was for the troops to aid "in quelling the disturbances" in that city. Despite repeated complaints to him from governors of the underdefended frontier states, Calhoun continued the military

This memorial dedicated to Denmark Vesey, located within the portico of Emanuel A.M.E. Church in Charleston, does not contain a likeness of the slave leader, as his appearance is unknown. Instead, a statuary group of African-American children is presented as listening to a sermon by Vesey promising liberation. (Kim Gissendanner)

The Charleston city jail for white prisoners, designed by Robert Mills and located opposite the Work House for slaves, was the first building visible to Vesey when he was led from his cell at dawn to be hanged on July 2, 1822. (Kim Gissendanner)

Robert Mills Manor, a public housing project built in the late 1930s, occupies the ground where the Work House—site of Denmark Vesey's imprisonment before his execution—once was located. (Kim Gissendanner)

Line Street, which traverses an economically depressed area north of the historic district of Charleston, is where twenty-two of Vesey's coconspirators were hanged on a single day in 1822. (Kim Gissendanner)

The "Ashley Avenue Oak," from which, according to local black tradition, Denmark Vesey was hanged, was cut down by the city of Charleston in the early 1970s. This younger tree was planted in a traffic median to replace it. The smaller oak still is habitually referred to as "Denmark Vesey's tree" by black residents along the avenue. (Kim Gissendanner)

Artist's rendering of Denmark Vesey's house and shop at 56 Bull Street, Charleston. (It was 20 Bull Street during Vesey's lifetime.) The house has continued to be a private residence in the twentieth century, and has been designated a National Historic Landmark by the National Park Service. (Dick Mitchell)

DICK MITCHELL '95

WEDNESDAY MORNING, JULY 3, 1822.

The Treaty with France, published in this morning's *Courier*, is copied from the *National Intelligencer* of the 26th ult. in which paper it appears both in French and English —but as we have no *accents* amongst our types, it was impossible for us to give it correctly in the French language. In the French copy, the signature of M. HYDE DE NEUVILLE precedes that of Mr. ADAMS.

Execution.—DENMARK VESEY, (a free black man) ROLLA, BATTEAU, NED, PETER, and JESSE, (slaves) convicted of an attempt to raise an insurrection in this State, were executed, pursuant to sentence, yesterday morning, between the hours of 6 and 8 o'clock.

Officers of the *Charleston Bible Society,* for 1822—3 :

Gen. C. C. PINCKNEY, President.
Rev. Dr. FURMAN, Senior Vice-President.
Rev. Dr. PALMER, Vice President.
Rev. Mr. BACHMAN, Vice-President.
THOMAS LOWNDES, Vice-President.
Rev. A. GIBBES, Corresponding Secretary.
Rev. A. BUIST, Corresponding Secretary.
T. S. GRIMKE, Recording Secretary.
WM. PAYNE, Treasurer.
Managers.—Rev. Messrs. Galluchat, Boice, and Myers ; Messrs. George Macauhy, John Haslett, D. Ravenel, T. Ford, James Jervey, Wm. Rouse, Mitchell, Harper, T. Corbett, T. Flemming, and J. Legare.
James R. Schenck, *Librarian.*

The execution of Denmark Vesey and five of his coconspirators on July 2, 1822, was not the leading news item the following day in the Charleston Courier.

This portrayal of Denmark Vesey addressing his followers, with his back toward the viewer, was installed for public display at Charleston's municipal auditorium in 1976. The painting was stolen shortly after its dedication, but was brought back anonymously to the auditorium after Charleston's mayor made a personal appeal that it be returned, and not be destroyed or vandalized. (Painting by Dorothy B. Wright. Photograph by Alan Hawes)

strengthening of Charleston throughout his tenure. As a consequence, Charleston by 1860 was perhaps the most fortified city in the United States, with guns that could point both inward and outward.

Charleston also prepared a uniquely institutional defense. In 1822, the city government, noting the inadequacy of a nightly watch, petitioned the state government for the establishment of an arsenal, or "citadel," independent of the city's police force, to protect the white citizens against "an enemy in the bosom of the state." By 1825, construction was under way, and, by 1841, by an act of the state legislature, the Citadel was established as South Carolina's state military academy. Cadets from local families drilled weekly under arms in an intimidating show of white force to Charleston's black community.

Two months after Abraham Lincoln's first election to the presidency, the U.S. government dispatched the USS *Star of the West* to replenish the besieged federal garrison at Fort Sumter in Charleston Harbor. Concealed among the sandy dunes on the ship's approach to the harbor was a well-armed force from the local military academy. The teenaged boys loaded their howitzer artillery pieces and lined up their sights on the *Star of the West*. Almost thirty-nine years after the execution of Denmark Vesey, on January 9, 1861, cadets from the Citadel fired the opening shots of the American Civil War.

INTENDANT JAMES HAMILTON never lived to see the civil war he had, in part, helped to provoke. Within the internecine world of Charleston politics, he had made enemies, unrelated to his role in the Vesey affair. By the mid-1850s, the "hero of Charleston" was out of public office, and his ambitions for the nation's vice-presidency unrealized. Despite the slaves and plantations acquired from his wife's family, he was in financial difficulties. His family and friends were further embarrassed by Hamilton's recent conversion to Spiritualism, by which he held "nightly communications" with the apparition of the dead John C. Calhoun, who assured him that the states' rights principles he had so revered in the U.S. Congress were also honored "in the other world."

In 1857, Hamilton decided to recover his fortunes by traveling to the expanding slave plantations of east Texas, perhaps with an eye toward returning in financial triumph to Charleston after a successful management of his family's western properties. Less than one day out from New Orleans, the ship on which he was traveling struck another vessel and began to sink. According to survivors, Hamilton appeared on deck, drew a pistol, and ordered the other men to help the white ladies. Moments later, a great wave crashed over the ship's deck, sweeping Hamilton overboard to certain death. His body was never recovered. His grave is as anonymous and illimitable as that of any unknown dead black man tossed overboard from the decks of a South Atlantic slaver.

CHAPTER EIGHT

The Darkness of Slavery: Denmark Vesey as a Historical Figure

When at length the King of Terrors approached, he shrieked in utter agony of spirit, "Oh, the darkness of blackness, the black imps, I can see them all around me—take them away!"
    —Theodore Weld, on the death of a southern slaveholder,
                    American Slavery As It Is, *1839*

Denmark Vesey smiles with pleasure from another century,
Black shadows on the empty streets . . .
                    —Charleston poet and resident Alice Cabiness,
                    on the city's imposition of martial law, 1969

"REMEMBER DENMARK VESEY of Charleston," Frederick Douglass urged potential recruits to the famous "Glory" Fifty-fourth Massachusetts Regiment of black volunteers on March 2, 1863. "Liberty won by white men would lose half its luster. Who would be free themselves must strike the blow." Douglass's appeal to the memory of Vesey gives evidence that his life and intended insurrection were not forgotten, at least at the level of public discourse, by whites and free blacks throughout the first half of the nineteenth century. Indeed, as some in the nation des-

perately sought to avoid by compromise—and others precipi-
tously rushed toward—the "impending" crisis of 1861–65, Vesey's
name was frequently involved as a historical figure. Just as in the
twentieth century, when he would again be invoked as a literary
symbol, Vesey was remembered as a figure of black pride and of
white fears.

The white fear of domestic blacks' remembering Denmark
Vesey was first directed, however, at the Caribbean Republic of
Haiti. Blacks on the island had successfully rebelled under the
generalship of the ex-slave Toussaint L'Ouverture, and in 1804,
the former island of St. Domingue was declared the Republic of
Haiti. By 1823, a year after Vesey's execution, the question arose as
to whether the United States government should establish diplomatic relations with the black republic. Opinions split along sec-
tional lines, with newspapers and legislators from roughly north
of Pennsylvania in favor of recognition. But to many southern
slaveholders and publishers, to receive the Haitian ambassador
was perceived as an implicit approval of the legitimacy of slave
revolt, and as an incendiary reminder to domestic blacks of the
near-success of Denmark Vesey at Charleston only twelve
months earlier. "Could the prejudices of some, and the, perhaps,
just fears of others be quieted?" asked the influential (Baltimore)
Niles Register on September 27, 1823. The newspaper answered its
own question in an indirect but unmistakable reference to the
Vesey plot. "We think not. The time has not yet come for a
surrender of our feelings about color, nor is it fitting, at any
time, that the public safety should be endangered." President
James Monroe chose to delay indefinitely action on Haitian
recognition.

Charlestonians remembered the first wave of white refugees
from St. Domingue to their city in 1793, who brought with them
Creole-speaking slaves and stories of rape by blacks and other
racial horrors. And they recalled how Denmark Vesey briefly had
worked in the island's sugar fields as a boy, how he had recruited

the Charleston district's French Negroes to his plans, how Vesey could speak French fluently, and how he purportedly had dispatched a letter to President Jean-Pierre Boyer of Haiti, asking for possible refuge and military aid in the South Carolina black revolt. (At the 1822 trials, the city court had required two of the accused slaves, Louis Remoussin and Peirault Strohecker, to speak together in a creolized French, proving to the judges' satisfaction that the possibility of a conspiracy existed among the French Negroes.) Hence, when diplomatic relations with Haiti were again considered by the U.S. government in 1826, southerners perceived the issue both as an attack upon the institution of slavery and as an attempt to befriend Denmark Vesey's murderous Caribbean ally. "The question of slavery is one, in all its bearings, of extreme delicacy," U.S. Senator Robert L. Hayne of South Carolina asserted in a speech on Haitian recognition in 1826. "To touch it at all is to violate our most sacred rights, to put in jeopardy our dearest interests, the peace of our country, *the safety of our families, our altars, and our firesides* [author's emphasis]." Hayne concluded: "I consider our rights in that species of property as not even open to discussion, either here or elsewhere." The United States did not grant diplomatic recognition to the Republic of Haiti until 1863.

Yet, the issues in which the memories of Denmark Vesey were most publicly involved were the two great domestic attempts of nineteenth-century America to avoid a civil war over "that species of property," otherwise known as black human beings. These were the Missouri Compromise of 1820 and the Compromise of 1850. The former was like a bone stuck in the throat of the developing nation, endangering both northerners and southerners alike. "We are sorry to see that a discussion of the hateful 'Missouri question' is likely to be revived," the (Washington, D.C.) *National Intelligencer* observed on August 31, 1822, "in consequence of its supposed effect in promoting the servile insurrection in South Carolina." Within a month of Vesey's execution, his attempted revolt had instigated just such a "revival" of the "question."

The Missouri Compromise occupied much of the nation's political attention in the years 1819–20, just when Vesey was recruiting his lieutenants in the slave revolt; and printed speeches by one of the Compromise's chief critics, Senator Rufus King of New York, were read by Vesey in Charleston and secretly distributed by him among his literate followers. The compromise was an attempt by a national southerner, Speaker of the House Henry Clay, to mollify the Deep South slaveholders, while at the same time limiting the expansion of slavery into the new states organized from the territories of Thomas Jefferson's Louisiana Purchase. By an act of Congress in 1820, slavery was prohibited north of latitude 36°30'. South of that line, slavery was to be left unchallenged by the federal government. As a further concession to the continuation of southern congressional power, Missouri was admitted to the Union as a slaveholding state. Clay's timely compromise forestalled a civil war, but it pleased neither northern abolitionists nor southern congressional radicals, who resented any restrictions on their region's national expansion of black slavery. But perhaps the most disturbed was the aging resident of Monticello who had peacefully obtained these territories for the United States. Jefferson—in an unwittingly apt image for Vesey's plans to create an alarm of fire and kill the whites of Charleston as they rushed from their houses—wrote in 1820 that he had heard the news of the Missouri Compromise "like a firebell in the night, [which] awakened and filled me with terror. . . . A geographical line, coinciding with a marked principle, moral and political, once conceived and held up to the angry passions of men will never be obliterated; and each new invitation will mark it deeper and deeper."

Within a mere two years after the Missouri Compromise's passage, the angry passions of Vesey and his judges had inflamed and deeply scored the national dividing line between free and slave. By late 1822, James Hamilton had published the confession of one of the thirty-five condemned, Jack Purcell, spoken "a few moments preceding his execution." According to Hamilton, Purcell confessed to him that Vesey "one day brought me a speech which he told me had been delivered in Congress by a Mr. King [Rufus King of New York] on the subject of slavery; he told me that this Mr. King was the black man's friend, that Mr. King had declared that he would continue to speak, write, and publish pamphlets against slavery for as long as he lived, until the southern states consented to emancipate their slaves, for that slavery was a disgrace to the country." Among his illiterate followers, according to the *Official Report* of his judges, Vesey frequently had declared "that Congress has made us free," and that Charleston masters were maliciously withholding this knowledge from their black slaves.

To congressional southerners such as Hayne and Hamilton, the implications of the Missouri Compromise for the Vesey plot and the prospect of future slave insurrections were clear. Any conditions put upon the expansion of black slavery would only incite incendiary revolts in the states of slavery's origin, and whites and blacks both must understand that the United States was, legally and irrevocably, a slaveholding union. Or, in Hayne's words cited just above, the constitutional right of any white citizen of the United States to buy or sell black human beings was "not even open to discussion, either here or elsewhere." Consequently, when the acquisition of new western territories required the negotiation of a new national compromise in 1850, intransigent white southerners in Congress fought for the unconditional extension of slavery to these areas and succeeded in getting much of what they wanted. The territories of New Mexico and Utah were organized with no restrictions placed upon black slavery, and the provisions of the Fugitive Slave Act were to be rigorously enforced in the northern free states, thus legally requiring the return to southern bondage of runaway slaves. The Compromise of 1850 almost perfectly realized the dream of white South Carolinians of the generation of 1822: the expansion of a black slave empire toward the Pacific Ocean, and the forced recognition by the northern states of the de jure permanence of U.S. slavery. Manumission of slaves also was made much more difficult in South Carolina, requiring a special act by the state legislature. There were to be no more Denmark Veseys.

As Henry Clay, John C. Calhoun, and Daniel Webster negotiated congressional passage of the Compromise of 1850 in the late fall, conspicuously absent in the debate was any collective voice of the nearly 3 million black Americans held in legal bondage that year. But in a patent attempt to influence this legislation, there appeared in early 1850 a pamphlet entitled *The Late Contemplated Insurrection in Charleston, S.C.*, published anonymously in New York State by "A Colored American." (Its author is believed to have been either the fugitive slave Henry Bibb or the free black editor Thomas Hamilton.) Denmark Vesey and the thirty-four others executed after his attempt were publicly described in this pamphlet as a "band of patriots," whose love of individual liberty had been "made holy by the American Revolution." The anonymous "colored" author particularly castigated the change in South Carolina's manumission laws, which made impossible the accumulation by slaves of "hard earnings at night work, for the express purpose of purchasing their freedom." Under such circumstances of bondage, the author argued, black revolt in South Carolina and elsewhere was both an historical inevitability and a moral imperative. Also, in 1859, Martin R. Delany, a free black who was an early advocate of pan-Africanism and the voluntary emigration of U.S. blacks to Africa, published *Blake, or the Huts of America*, a fictionalized tour of the slave communities of the Deep South. Delany described fugitive blacks as still "remembering Denmark Vesey" as an example of black resistance.

But for the majority of whites and blacks in the South, particularly in Charleston, the business of daily life and relations between master and slave continued unchallenged throughout the late 1840s and the 1850s. In Charleston, the slave Peter Prioleau, who had been the first to betray Vesey's plot, had been freed by a special act of the legislature on Christmas Day, 1822. He also received a lifetime annual pension of $100. Prioleau was soon afterward accepted into the free mulatto and black slaveholding elite of the city. In the U.S. census of 1840, he was reported as the owner in Charleston of seven slaves, including a married couple, Alfred and Lavinia Sanders, and their two-year-old son. In 1849, Prioleau, apparently needing money, sold the Sanderses' son to another master for $235.

THE MOST DETAILED nineteenth-century remembrance of Denmark Vesey was published in June 1861, two months after federal troops surrendered Fort Sumter. The author was Thomas Higginson, a descendant of New England clerisy and a political defender of both Frederick Douglass and John Brown. One of the first white officers at the start of the Civil War to advocate the right of blacks to enlist in the U.S. Army, Higginson accepted assignment in 1862 to the Sea Islands south of Charleston, where the Union military had managed to establish a small force. There he helped drill, and accepted the colonelcy of, the first black regiment in the U.S. Army, the First South Carolina Volunteers. Higginson, a year earlier, as an example of black military competency and desire for freedom, had published in the *Atlantic Monthly* the first short biography of Denmark Vesey.

Higginson seized the opportunity, particularly in the postwar reprintings of his "Denmark Vesey," to include corroborating details from black and white South Carolinians who still remembered the Vesey plot. "There is no [military] reason why they should not have taken the city," the future colonel wrote of Vesey and his conspirators, except for the unforeseeable circumstances of Peter Prioleau's and George Wilson's betrayals. Higginson confirmed that both guns and over a "hundred pikes and daggers" had been secreted in anticipation of the night of revolt, and that Vesey's tactical plans to seize the city's state and federal armories had been professionally thought through to achieve their objectives. (Interestingly, Higginson mentions the persistent rumor that, despite the city's news blackout of the plot's discovery and the arrival of military reinforcements, "the Secretary of War was informed of the plot, even including some details of the plan and the leader's name, before it was known in Charleston.") Higginson, privy to blacks who were more willing sources of information to him than to any previous white author, perhaps solved the mystery of why so many weapons were described by Vesey's coconspirators but so few were produced at the trials. Immediately after the arrests of Vesey and his major conspirators, Higginson was told, the pikes, spears, and other weapons assembled by Vesey and his cohorts were "buried in coffins on Sullivan's Island" by blacks on that coastal island for their use in future revolts. Higginson deferred to the official accounts of white authorities, however, in his restating that Vesey had been hanged at Blake's Lands, and not, as black oral tradition always maintained, from the Ashley Avenue Oak, which was much closer to the city.

Higginson was determined, however, that his readers in 1861 recognize the central fact of Denmark Vesey as a historical figure: black slavery, however benevolently defined or nationally comprised by the U.S. Congress, had made revolt and civil war a certainty. The military response at Charleston to Vesey's threat and that city's violent willingness to resist federal authority, he wrote, at least demonstrated "that rarest of qualities" in the slaveholding city, "a willingness to look facts in the face."

Subsequently, three thousand exuberant blacks and a few hundred whites gathered at Charleston Harbor to face a historical fact on April 14, 1865: On that date, Good Friday, Secretary of

War Edwin Stanton ordered the U.S. flag to be officially raised over Fort Sumter for the first time since the fort's surrender in 1861. The day was a jubilee for both Charleston's former slaves and the black federal troops then occupying the city. (The news of President Lincoln's assassination that night did not reach Charleston until the following week.) "The Star-Spangled Banner" was played, and as the same tattered U.S. flag that had fluttered over Fort Sumter during the 1861 bombardment was once more raised, a roar of joy went up from the crowd of blacks assembled along the harbor and from a flotilla of boats gathered in the water around the fort. Among the invited guests aboard a Union gunboat was Denmark Vesey's son, Robert Vesey.

Although Robert Vesey may have been born a free individual, the life of any black in early-nineteenth-century Charleston was lived in a world of dangerous legal and racial ambiguities. The city directories of the 1840s through the 1850s do not list a Robert Vesey as a free black resident of Charleston. Nor does his name appear on any of the city's antebellum tax rolls for free blacks; in a direct response to the Vesey plot, the city of Charleston aggressively had collected a special tax from free black residents within its parishes, and although the surname Vesey appears occasionally on the records for the 1840s and 1850s, there is no listing for a Robert. (Susan Vesey, who was recorded as cohabiting with Denmark Vesey at 20 Bull Street in 1822, disappears from the tax rolls after that year.) The *Official Report* of his father's revolt does not record Robert Vesey as among those arrested or interrogated during the trials, but his civil status from 1822 to 1860 is uncertain. At some time after 1860, the last year for which the free black tax records are extant, and by which year Robert Vesey surely would have reached his physical majority, the names recorded in the manuscript under *V* were either lost or destroyed.

Robert Vesey's documented presence at Fort Sumter in 1865, and his years thereafter at Charleston, represent the last tangible history of the flesh of his revolutionary father. Vesey exceeded his father's carpentry skills by becoming a noted contractor and practical architect; and, in 1865, when the A.M.E. congregation collected money to replace the church building burned down after Denmark Vesey's execution, Robert Vesey was selected as the builder. But the family name and living memory of Denmark Vesey declined with the passing of this generation of black Charlestonians. The U.S. census of 1870 listed only Sarah Vesey, sixty years of age, and Hannah Vesey, age seventy, as living in Charleston. Sarah Vesey, identified by the census as a mulatto, was a twelve-year-old girl in 1822; Hannah Vesey, identified as a black, was a twenty-two-year-old woman in the summer of Denmark Vesey's attempted revolt. By 1880, the name had disappeared entirely from the census of blacks and whites then living in Charleston.

DENMARK VESEY has been remembered in the twentieth century in large part through the writings of such scholars of slavery as Archibald H. Grimké, Herbert Aptheker, and John Hope Franklin. Each emphasized the extraordinary nature of the Vesey plot's comprehensiveness and its historical consequences, but their research was often published in journals of small circulation. The first literary attempt in the twentieth century to present Denmark Vesey to a larger audience was, ironically, authored by the widow of an aristocratic white Charlestonian. Dorothy Heyward earlier had collaborated with her husband, DuBose Heyward, in writing the popular play *Porgy*. Its theatrical production had been considered among the accomplishments of the Harlem Renaissance of the 1920s in employing black actors, and its plot provided the inspiration for George Gershwin's later opera, in 1935, *Porgy and Bess*. In the fall of 1948, Dorothy Heyward wrote and aided in the New York Theatre Guild production of her five-act play based upon Denmark Vesey's attempted revolt, *Set My People Free*.

Set My People Free had a short run to mixed reviews. The drama critic for the *New York Times* noted that the actual history of the Vesey plot "supplies the materials for some of the most exhilarating acting of the season," but he complained "there is almost a formula for Negro plays. It derives from 'Porgy,' of which Mrs. Heyward was co-author, and it includes spirituals, superstitions, incantation, and lithographic crowd scenes." But this play also may have been rejected by a wider audience for reasons unrelated to its possible literary shortcomings. Even more than 120 years after his execution, Denmark Vesey may have been perceived as too revolutionary a figure for popular acceptance or theatrical celebration.

The same year as the first production of Dorothy Heyward's play was also the threshold of the Cold War and the anniversary of the first modern attempt at civil rights legislation, introduced in the 1947–48 sessions of Congress. These historical events found their way into the Vesey review. The *Times* critic in that newspaper's evaluation of *Set My People Free* sought in his review "to quiet the nerves of theatregoers who may think they are seeing the handbook of political revolution by a minority group. For the secret meetings, the pledge to obey the leader's commands, the training of conspirators and the ruthless renunciation of humane considerations—all have a familiar ring now."

Such words were also to have an ominously familiar resonance in the official police denunciations of the following decades, when Denmark Vesey once more would be perceived as an important figure of black liberation and his name again shouted by blacks in political protest. Writing in 1959, Stanley Elkins noted that Denmark Vesey—the "leading spirit of the 1822 plot at Charleston"—had, like all other near-successful slave insurrectionists of the nineteenth century, gained his most dedicated following in urban centers. The police reaction to reports of slave insurrections in southern antebellum cities was, Elkins wrote, to perceive them "like Communist conspiracies in our own day." The comparison was apt, and prescient. In the 1960s, Denmark Vesey again would be remembered, not only in scholarly journals and on the stage but also in the streets and jail cells of the nation's cities.

The first half of that decade witnessed a revival of scholarly interest in Denmark Vesey. In 1964, Antioch Press published the first book-length study of Vesey, *Insurrection in South Carolina*, by John Lofton, detailing the effects of the Charleston plot upon passage of the Negro Seamen Act of 1822. Foremost among other articles that decade was the treatise published in a 1966 edition of *Negro Digest*, "Remembering Denmark Vesey: Agitator or Insurrectionist?" by Sterling Stuckey, a cofounder of the Chicago Amistad Society. Stuckey described his biographical subject as a progenitor of the civil rights leaders of the 1960s, and he emphasized that "Vesey's example must be regarded as one of the most courageous ever to threaten the racist foundations of America." But the most potent evocation of Vesey was in the city of his planned insurrection, Charleston, in 1969, after a year of political assassinations and racial riots across the United States. In this historic southern city, in what the *New York Times* then described as "the country's tensest civil rights struggle," the name of Denmark Vesey again became a rallying cry for black citizens, who were led by the recently widowed wife of Dr. Martin Luther King, Jr., against the city's and state's police forces.

The confrontations began in the city in late March, when twelve black domestic workers were fired by the state government from the Medical College Hospital at Charleston for union organizing and for petitioning their administrators for a raise to $1.30 per hour. Their cause was championed by Coretta Scott King, Andrew Young, and the Reverend Ralph Abernathy of the Southern Christian Leadership Conference. In response, five thousand heavily armed National Guardsmen were ordered into the city by the state government and a nightly curfew was enforced. On April 26, in an act of patent symbolism to both the blacks and the whites of the city, Abernathy addressed 2,500 strike sympathizers assembled for a protest march toward downtown Charleston from the Morris Brown A.M.E. Church, named for the free black who had been exiled from South Carolina and whose church building at Charleston had been burned after Vesey's attempted insurrection. On April 30, Mrs. King led a group of demonstrators estimated at fifteen hundred toward the hospital from the Emanuel A.M.E. Church, the "mother church" of that black congregation in South Carolina and the site on which Robert Vesey had constructed the building after the Union occupation in 1865. In both cases, the modern demonstrations were met by National Guardsmen with loaded rifles, fixed bayonets, and an armored personnel carrier to turn aside what the local newspaper described as black "rebels." Mrs. King was spared arrest, but Abernathy and over nine hundred other demonstrators were jailed. More than a century after his execution, cries of "Remember Denmark Vesey!" were shouted by protesters in the streets of Charleston.

The wage dispute eventually was resolved by HEW Secretary Robert Finch to the satisfaction of hospital workers and the state government. There was also the added incentive to the white city government of avoiding any further disruption of the important tourist season. The historic district of Charleston had emerged during the early 1970s as one of the most popular spring destinations on the East Coast for American and European visitors, an economic fact of great importance to both black and white residents of the city. As a further concession to black residents, a portrait of Denmark Vesey was hung by the city in 1976 in the municipal auditorium.

But the desire to subordinate—or to obliterate—the historical memory of Denmark Vesey in Charleston was always just below the surface. Ashley Avenue, where there long stood a large oak tree from which, according to local black tradition, Vesey had been hanged, became a major thoroughfare as a result of the city's economic expansion. The avenue was widened in order to accommodate increased automobile traffic, and the local chapter of the Jaycees began to complain that the tree was a traffic hazard. In 1973, the "Ashley Avenue Oak" was declared diseased, and taken down by the city. According to a local historical society, portions of the tree were then laminated and fashioned into desks and other "home memorabilia" for white residences.

CHAPTER NINE

———— ⋙◉⋘ ————

Remembering Denmark Vesey as a Black Leader

> *I sell you no phony forgiveness.*
> —*Ralph Ellison,* Invisible Man, *1952*

THERE ARE NO PUBLIC high schools in this country named for Denmark Vesey. The denial to him of this most prosaic of honors results less from the official suppression of Vesey's aspirations than from the failure of contemporary blacks and whites to agree among themselves on Vesey's place among African-American leaders. Like his fellow black Caribbean in the early twentieth century, Marcus Garvey, Vesey urged the economic self-sufficiency of U.S. blacks and the justice of their emigration to Africa. Unlike Garvey, Vesey considered murder, arson, and looting as legitimate means of achieving these goals. He was undeniably a man capable of compassion, and at times he employed, along with other blacks, the vocabulary of the Christian faith. Yet he can also be seen as a precursor of the terrible practitioners of twentieth-century genocide. When questioned by his followers on the necessity of killing white infants and children on the night of his revolution, Vesey's response was, simply, "What [is] the use of killing the louse and leaving the nit?"

To most whites aware of his existence, Denmark Vesey occupies historically a place that is sometimes near the moral acceptability of Martin Luther King, Jr., and frequently beyond the mainstream apostasy of Malcolm X. Vesey was, in a sense, a "purer" leader than either. In his life, there is no single moment of excoriating hope, as in Dr. King's letter from the Birmingham jail in 1963, or of black self-definition, as during Malcolm X's incarceration in Massachusetts State Prison. In Vesey's life, both moments were always there, even apparently during his adolescence aboard a South Atlantic slaver.

For blacks, any historical celebration of Denmark Vesey is complicated by the fact that he was much more a despotic leader than an egalitarian populist. There is an unmistakable *haughtiness* in Vesey's view of Charleston's other blacks. "You deserve to remain slaves," he dismissively told those blacks who bowed on the street to whites, and who, unlike the free Vesey, had no legal protection if they refused to do so. Even disallowing his judges' descriptions of him, Vesey during the conspiracy trials is in the testimonies of slaves referred to more frequently in terms of fear than of racial fraternity; and even though some of the convicted, perhaps in the hope of mitigating their sentences, publicly renounced Vesey after his execution, they continued in court to speak of him in words that intimated a sense of awe. As one of the convicted told his astonished judges, he feared Vesey "more than he feared his God."

These characteristics do not diminish Vesey historically as an important African-American leader. They mean simply that he must be accepted on his own terms, just as he insisted he be accepted during his lifetime. His intimidating physical presence, his intellectual strength, his free status, his international background and religious experiences—all contributed to Vesey's sense of himself as the personal embodiment of black self-sufficiency and independence. This historical force of his personality, even after his death, insists that others also see him so.

Martin R. Delany, the free black who briefly memorialized Vesey in the 1859 novel *Blake*, first proclaimed him publicly to whites and blacks in 1865 as an example of negritude leadership. Delany, who had received a Union military commission and was to head the South Carolina Freedmen's Bureau, addressed an assembly of black and white Charlestonians at Zion Presbyterian Church on May 12, 1865, within a month of the flag-raising ceremony at Fort Sumter. The purpose of the meeting, as announced in the city newspaper by Major Delany and other officers of the occupation force, was to discuss "the condition of the people released from rebel tyranny."

Delany chose to devote his remarks exclusively to reminding his audience "of the great insurrectionary movement in South Carolina under the lead of Denmark Vesey." He noted that the plot had been betrayed by a mulatto, George Wilson, and that such incidents were "the cause of prejudice existing among the different classes of the colored people." It was in militant opposition to just such a divide-and-conquer strategy against blacks, Delany stated, that Denmark Vesey had given his life. "It was a scheme of that class of slaveholders," Delany said, "to make confidants of the mulattos [*sic*] and cut off so much strength of the blacks." Delany told his audience that he "hoped this prejudice would now all disappear with the slavery that had gone before it."

Vesey presented himself to his followers as the rallying spokesman for a new doctrine of negritude. "We must unite together as the Santo Domingo people did," he told both his black and his mulatto recruits, "never to betray one another, and to die before we would tell upon one another." Vesey chose only a few mulatto recruits, but at least three, Jacob Stagg, Pharo Thompson, and Jack Purcell, were judged by the city to have been so actively committed to his planned insurrection that they were among the thirty-five conspirators hanged. Even at the demotic level of "Gullah Jack" Pritchard's talismans and charms distributed among the Ibo and Gullah recruits, Vesey carefully emphasized the greater potency of black cultural, racial, and political unity. The powers of Gullah Jack's magic, they were told, "would not protect him from the treachery of his own color."

In his relations with the blacks whom he judged worthy not to remain slaves, Vesey sought to empower them with the literacy and economic self-sufficiency of the city's free mulatto class, as a separate and independent people. Here he anticipated the economic and political aspirations of Malcolm X for blacks during the early 1960s. "We must not stand with hands in our pockets," Vesey often told potential slave recruits—meaning that they must not, like the free mulattoes, depend upon the personal benevolence of whites for private manumissions, or upon such political gradualism as the Missouri Compromise, or even upon the aggressive liberalism of the northern abolitionists. "I knew Denmark Vesey," one black among many testified under duress to the city court. "I was one day on horseback going to market when I met him on foot; he asked if I was satisfied in my present situation." When the slave replied that he was not, Vesey told him "Go, and buy a spelling book and read the fable of Hercules and the Wagoner, whose wagon was stalled, and he began to pray, and Hercules said, 'You fool, put your shoulder to the wheel, whip up the horses, and the wagon will be pulled out.'" The moral of the fable, Vesey then told him, was "that if we did not put our hand to the work and deliver ourselves, that we would never come out of slavery."

Vesey's innate distrust of a black bourgeoisie supported by whites, his insistence upon black separatism and economic independence, and his advocacy of "by any means necessary" tactics to achieve these goals prefigure another black leader for whom at least some public schools have been named. "Integration is not good for either side," Malcolm X told a largely white Harvard Law School audience in 1961. "God has declared that these twenty million ex-slaves must have a home of their own." In the tradition of Martin Delany and Denmark Vesey, Malcolm X seriously considered the voluntary emigration of U.S. blacks to

Africa, or at least their economic, political, and cultural support of an independent African nation, analogous to such support by U.S. Jewish citizens to the nation of Israel. "The only real solution to our problem, just as the Honorable Elijah Muhammad has taught us," Malcolm X told his shocked audience, "is to go back to our homeland and live among our own people and develop it so we'll have an independent nation of our own."

The iconoclasm of both Denmark Vesey and Malcolm X is well beyond the accepted American pieties of assimilation, integration, and equality of races and cultures; but their acknowledged leadership positions are invaluable in forcing both white and black Americans to reexamine their true commitments to these pieties when the alternatives are presented as either the national shame of a black hegira or the horrors of racial war. Malcolm X quoted to his Harvard audience Revelation 13:10, a biblical verse with which Denmark Vesey, judging by his motivations and his planned actions, probably was intimately familiar. The verse tells the oppressed not to expect mercy, and the oppressors not to hope to escape retribution: "If any one is to be taken captive, to captivity he goes; if anyone slays with the sword, with the sword must he be slain."

In the evidence of his planned revolt, however, Vesey does not reveal himself to have been completely a pan-Africanist, such as Delany or Garvey, or a supra-Africanist, such as Professor Leonard Jeffries of the City College of New York. Despite the forced presence in the Charleston District of perhaps the greatest U.S. concentration in 1822 of first-generation African slaves, Vesey included few of their number among his primary coconspirators. As a revolutionary leader, he was a prophet of the Enlightenment of the eighteenth century, during which he gained his physical majority and his literacy. Like many of the white architects of the American Revolution, Vesey believed in political action by autocracy, and not in the romantic herrenvolk of the nineteenth and twentieth centuries. Of the thirty-five conspirators who confessed or were judged to have been so deeply involved in Vesey's plot that the city justified their hanging, only four were officially described as "Africans." This number among his primary coconspirators is only one greater than the number of mulattoes, a racial group toward whom Vesey had ambiguous feelings at best. (The classifications of mulatto, African, or "country born" usually were scrupulously recorded by the white judges during the trials of Vesey and his coconspirators.) One first-generation African slave, Monday Gell, born an Ibo and picked by Vesey to recruit among that linguistic and national community of blacks in South Carolina, chose to preserve his life and turn state's evidence after Vesey's execution. Gell provided the convicting testimony against many of the other twenty-nine blacks who were hanged after the six executions on July 2.

Vesey's autocracy—his sense of his own powerful gift of leadership—apparently precluded his accepting as his equal any other African or free black male in the planned liberation of Charleston's slaves. Peter Poyas, an economically independent slave who exercised his own will in terms of leadership and who at times comforted Vesey, was nevertheless a slave. There is no record of black females being recruited to the insurrection by either Vesey or Poyas. "I beg you won't take up Sarah, for no woman knows anything about it," the defendant William Paul pleaded to his judges during the conspiracy trials. The Sarah to whom Paul referred was almost certainly a stepdaughter with that name from Denmark Vesey's marriage to Beck Vesey. (This stepdaughter may be the sixty-year-old woman listed as Sarah Vesey in the census of 1870.) If, indeed, no women of color were invited by Denmark Vesey into the plot, then he had denied to himself a group of recruits who could have provided invaluable intelligence to his revolt; Beck Vesey, for instance, despite estrangement from her husband, kept her separate household "near the Intendant's," in Paul's description, and she was well located for domestic spying on the Hamilton household.

The stance toward the plot by Prince Graham, the only other free black solicited by Vesey to be a major military leader, also is instructive. Graham, when first approached by one of Vesey's subordinates to lead a company of horsemen on the night of the revolt, declared "he was as willing as anybody." But when Vesey later called at Graham's house, he was told by the latter's wife, who answered the door, that Graham was not at home and "would have nothing to do with this conspiracy." After the discovery of the plot and the beginnings of an official persecution of Charleston's free blacks, Prince Graham, "at his own request, was transported to Africa," according to the account by the civic judges. His wife presumably accompanied him. Graham apparently had agreed with Vesey's agenda of a trans–low country black emigration to Africa, and he shared at least initially Vesey's passion for individual action. But there was apparently in Denmark Vesey's leadership an element that made Prince Graham and other free black men and women unwilling upon reflection to subordinate themselves to Vesey in matters of life and death.

Vesey's greatest success as a revolutionary black leader was not in the achievement of political negritude or the accomplishment of an African migration. However, faith in both remained as part of the African-American experiences of Christianity and Islam, as demonstrated in two centuries by spokesmen as diverse as Martin Delany at Zion Presbyterian Church and Malcolm X at Harvard University. The survival of this faith among both Christian and Muslim blacks in the United States contributed to Denmark Vesey's preeminence as a religious leader in his own lifetime, and, surprisingly, within some areas of twentieth-century theology.

The case for Vesey's profession of Islam, or at least some of its practices, is, as discussed in an earlier chapter, more circumstantial than explicitly documented. But it is undeniable that the Five Pillars of Islam—praying five times daily, aiding the unfortunate, disciplining oneself during Ramadan, traveling on a holy pilgrimage, and accepting the monotheism of Allah and the word of his prophet Muhammad—are within the mainstream of American history. Islamic blacks, perhaps 10 percent of the total slave population during Vesey's lifetime, arrived with the first white Anglican and Congregationalist settlers in the future United States. (The earliest record of the presence of Muslims in South Carolina was the petition, written in "Arabick," by two North Africans pleading with royal authorities for release from slavery in 1753.) A twentieth-century scholar who has made a study of Islamic slaves in the Georgia–South Carolina low country, Michael Gomez, has noted the attitude of what he terms "Muslim superiority," believed and perceived by both slaveholders and these slaves themselves, who frequently "were given more responsibility and privileges than other slaves." A sense of such superiority certainly existed in Denmark Vesey, who from his early years on had been elevated above other blacks even aboard a slave ship. The moral absolutism and personal expression of a "Muslim superiority" may explain why other free blacks found Denmark Vesey so off-putting, such as Prince Graham, who professed to be a Methodist.

Vesey's Christianity is better documented, but it is also more problematical for those who define that religion as the source of otherworldly deliverance and a loving forgiveness of one's enemies. It is certain that Vesey had a personal fascination with two biblical verses, which he habitually quoted to other blacks at his revolutionary meetings or at the religious classes he taught at the A.M.E. congregation. The first was Joshua 6:21: "And they utterly destroyed all that was in the city, both man and woman, young and old, and ox, and sheep, and ass, with the edge of the sword." The second was Exodus 9:1: "Then the Lord said to Moses, 'Go in to Pharaoh and say to him, "Thus says the Lord, the God of the Hebrews, 'Let my people go, that they may serve me.'"'" So well known and so repeated among low-country blacks was Vesey's biblical comparison of their bondage to the captivity of the Israelites that several twentieth-century scholars believe it to have been the genesis of a celebrated spiritual. "In time, the essence of Vesey's sermon would become stylized, like the structure of folk ballads," Marion Starkey wrote in 1964. The result of Vesey's sermon being repeated rhythmically and reduced to its essentials was, in the opinion of Starkley and Vincent Harding, the spiritual "Go Down Moses." Harding believes that this anonymously composed spiritual may first have been sung by Carolina blacks early in the nineteenth century as a way of covertly honoring Vesey and his cohorts. "Was it out there in the fields, late in the Carolina nighttime," Harding speculates, "that a voice first lifted the slow and halting melody?"

Vesey also made more direct use of a recruit's Christian faith on at least one occasion. Mary Beach recounted in her letters how she had heard one slave had been approached by Vesey to join in the revolt but had refused on the grounds of self-interest, as "his wife and children were free, and he lives as well as he could wish for himself." Vesey then returned with a Bible, according to Beach, and, citing the sacrifice and fellowship emphasized therein, told the recruit "that if he did not do it for himself, or had no reason, *he ought to do it for the sake of others* [author's emphasis]."

Thus, there appears to have been more than just a literal selectivity or a racial expediency in Vesey's participation as a black Christian. He is revered today as both a spiritual and a political champion of the A.M.E. church. (The only public statuary honoring Vesey is located at the Emanuel A.M.E. Church at Charleston, where a group of black children are portrayed listening to his sermons on liberation. The figures are protected against vandalism by heavy iron gates.) Within his lifetime, Vesey also exercised an influence upon black church members other than the A.M.E. congregation in a way that had theological implications for both his century and the next.

Shortly after Vesey's arrest in the summer of 1822, white members of the liberal Independent Congregational Circular Church at Charleston were shocked to learn that several of their black church attendants, including the governor's trusted slave Rolla Bennett, had confessed to having participated in the conspiracy. Unlike the members of the former A.M.E. congregation, these blacks did not have the animus toward whites arising from their church building being locked and their ministers jailed. Instead, Vesey had impressed upon Rolla Bennett and others that "they ought to engage in the business" because their white Congregational minister, Dr. Benjamin Palmer, had "made catechism *different* for the Negroes." ("This was the fact," Mary Beach wrote her sister, "but the poor man did it to accommodate *their* understanding.") Eugene Genovese, a twentieth-century scholar of slavery, would recognize the church's imposition of a different statement of Christian belief as an example of what he also termed *accommodationism*: the documentable campaign of white slaveholders to inculcate blacks with a sense of the divine rightness of their servitude. More significantly, Denmark Vesey a century earlier had recognized this substitution for what it was, and he had convinced others to reject it and to act politically from unadulterated faith. To at least a handful of black Christians, Vesey was able to change a doctrine of accommodation into a text for liberation.

This religious aspect of Vesey's leadership remained buried in local church tradition until the decades in the present century following the assassinations of Malcolm X and Martin Luther King, Jr. Beginning in the 1970s and extending through the late 1990s, there emerged nationally a systemic theology in which the historical Denmark Vesey was interpreted as a preeminently Christian figure. This historical and scriptural exegesis became known as "Black Theology." Perhaps its most cogent explicator is James H. Cone, professor of theology at Union Theological Seminary in New York and the author of *Black Theology and*

Black Power, A Black Theology of Liberation, and *God of the Oppressed.* As a black child growing up in segregated Arkansas, Cone had observed in the weekly services at the Macedonia A.M.E. Church what Denmark Vesey had perceived in the worship of Charleston's A.M.E. congregation in 1816: that although slavery had vitiated many black families and encouraged the mutual exploitation of one another by people of color in their ceaseless struggle for survival, the black church remained a unique source of political and spiritual empowerment. As Cone eloquently writes:

> After being treated as things for six days of the week, black folk went to church on Sunday in order to affirm another definition of their humanity. . . . [T]hat was why they called one another Mr. and Mrs., or brother and sister. The value structures of the society were completely reversed in the church. The last became first in that the janitor became the chairman of the Steward Board and the maid became the president of the Stewardess Board Number One. Everybody became somebody, and there were no second-class people at Macedonia.

In his subsequent historical and theological studies, Cone became convinced that "the seminal Black Theology was the theology that secretly taught that God wanted Black people to be free. Our greatest fighters for freedom were religious leaders—Denmark Vesey, Nat Turner, David Walker, Henry Highland Garner, and others." Influenced both by the European theology of Karl Barth's "courage to be" and by the liberation theology of Roman Catholic priests in Latin America, Cone and other national theologians argued that the political empowerment of people of color and the recognition of a positive "blackness" of God were the fulfillment in twentieth-century history of the Christian logos. Denmark Vesey's near-success and his silence before his persecutors became an important example to these theologians of what they call "the theology of hope." Writing in 1974 of Vesey's and Poyas's commands of silence to their followers, one theologian interpreted their muteness in prison as a directive to twentieth-century black and white Christians to continue their revolutionary activism:

"Do not open your lips; die silent as you shall see me do." But is silence before the executioner the "last word"? Or is it a "new" and decisive word still to be spoken over these unfinished lives, in the common future ahead?

His remembrance among some Christians as a historical typology of Christ might have grimly amused Denmark Vesey, the terrible and haughty urban black revolutionary. Or perhaps not. Eighty-one years after Vesey's execution, W. E. B. Du Bois characterized the history of the African-American experience as the simultaneous possession of "two souls, two thoughts, two unreconciled strivings." This duality is central to Vesey's leadership—a free black who felt himself enslaved, a secular Enlightenment autocrat who was also a passionate religionist, a liberator of the oppressed and a potential murderer of the innocent. But if the passions of Vesey's existence cannot be forgiven, or even reconciled, in terms of black and white, they should at least be historically acknowledged. And such an obligation leads to the historical search for Vesey's gravesite.

POSTSCRIPT

A Personal Conclusion: Spartacus's List and the Search for Vesey's Grave

They all perished except 6000, who were captured and crucified along the entire road from Capua to Rome.
    —Appian of Alexander, "The War with Spartacus," C.E. 160

To the readers of American history, Denmark Vesey and Peter Poyas have commonly been but the shadows of names.
    —Colonel Thomas Higginson, United States Army,
        "Denmark Vesey," 1861

IN BOTH THE OLD WORLD and the New, the records of slave revolts are a testimony to the courage of human beings, but they also are evidence of the human unwillingness to accept laws of probability. Throughout the settlements of North America, from the colonial era to the late antebellum years, hundreds of attempted black slave revolts—including Denmark Vesey's—have been documented. They ranged in area from New York State to Louisiana. None was successful. During the four-hundred-year reign of a "sugar and slaves" economy in the Caribbean and the West Indies, serious revolts by Native American Indian and African slaves occurred in such colonies as Barbados, the

Virgin Islands, Jamaica, and British Guiana. Only one, in St. Domingue, succeeded.

The history of revolts against European slavery is no more encouraging. Two accounts of armed resistance have survived historically for more than two millennia. But these chronicles have been preserved, at least initially, not because they succeeded. Rather, the victors thought they would become more historically attractive by recording their success against people who sought to be free.

Both of these early revolts in European history were recorded in the classical literature of the Roman Republic, which, before the birth of Christ, enjoyed a three-hundred-year run as a prosperous slave economy, a fact often cited by nineteenth-century southern intellectuals. Foremost is the *Commentaries* on the Gallic Wars, written by Julius Caesar to advance his political career. Within its seven books, Caesar recounts how he militarily crushed the resistance of the English, Belgian, German, and French peoples to Roman enslavement. Particularly troublesome to Caesar was Dumnorix, "a man of supreme daring, a great favorite with the people because of his generosity, and eager for political change." Finally, in 53 B.C.E., Caesar dispatched a large detachment of Roman cavalry to kill Dumnorix, and, very likely, enticed this Gaul's personal bodyguard to betray him in exchange for preference among Rome's slave population. When Dumnorix's bodyguard deserted him, Caesar wrote, and the Roman cavalry started hacking at the Gallic chieftain with their short swords, "Dumnorix began to resist, fighting to defend himself and begging his followers to help him, all the while shouting again and again that he was a free man and the citizen of a free state." The pleas were unsuccessful. "In accordance with my instructions," Caesar wrote, "he was surrounded and killed."

Less than twenty years earlier, the institution of Western slavery faced its most serious challenge in the revolt of Spartacus, the Thracian slave gladiator. Escaping from captivity in 73 B.C.E.,

Spartacus initially collected about him a few hundred former gladiatorial slaves; by 71, he had organized an army of approximately ninety thousand ex-slaves from agricultural villas and cities, taught them to fight as a disciplined unit, and defeated two Roman armies sent against them. Spartacus's original plan had been to battle his way northward across the Alps and disperse his followers as free men and women into unsettled areas of Gaul. Persuaded against his best judgment to turn southward toward the "boot" of Italy, he was forced into a final stand by the competing aristocratic commanders of two separate Roman armies, Gnaeus Pompeius Magnus and Marcus Licinius Crassus. The latter was reputed to be the wealthiest man and the largest slaveholder in the Western world at that time. Spartacus was badly wounded and his forces were decisively defeated in a battle occurring in 71; thereafter, Pompey and Crassus vied with each other in mopping up the remnants of the slave army in order to determine which of them would win the honor of a triumphal march into Rome and election the following year to the consulship. Crassus was seized by a sudden political inspiration, however, which won him the consulship and a certain place in history. Taking six thousand prisoners of war from Spartacus's defeated army, he ordered them crucified along the entire length of the Via Appia Antica, the main highway that then ran in a straight line from Rome to the southern coast for 132 miles.

History, as George Orwell reminded us, is written by the winners. Today, tourists picnic underneath the celebrated Umbrian pines that grow along the length of the Via Appia, or enjoy the various small restaurants along the old Roman highway—not because these twentieth-century visitors are heartless but because there are no historical remnants of the six thousand slave rebels who once were tortured to death alongside the road's paving stones. But to those who have learned the buried history of such scenes, the human imagery is difficult to thrust from one's memory—Dumnorix being hacked to death all the while "shouting again and again that he was a free man," or Peter Poyas's acid response twenty centuries later to a more sinister slave totalitarianism: "I suppose you'll let me see my wife and family before I die?"

There is a desire, both instinctual and intellectual, to set the record straight, and to accumulate as much historical and biographical information as possible about those individuals who dared defy the impersonal forces of enslavement. This desire also is evidence of human unwillingness to accept laws of probability. Stephen Jay Gould, a twentieth-century Harvard professor of biology, has characterized such a phenomenon as what may be called "Spartacus's List," a desire for unattainable knowledge. "If, for some reason, I wanted a list of every rebel crucified with Spartacus along the Appian Way," Gould has written, "I could not acquire such a record because it doesn't now exist (and probably never did)."

The extinction of historical facts about those individuals who should be recorded as having defied the odds for human freedom seems to confirm the opinion of Vesey's judges on delivering his sentence of death: "You had, therefore, much to risk, and little to gain. From your age and experience, you *ought* to have known that success was impracticable." Much of Vesey's life, and the lives of his companions, have vanished into the historical uncertainty of a Spartacus's List. It is not confirmable whether Vesey was born in Africa or the West Indies; the site of his execution has been obliterated; his face is unknown; and what he or his companions thought or felt, we can gather only from the very rare occasions when they are recorded as having spoken their own words. But as his Charleston judges told Vesey more than a century ago, we *ought* to know. This obligation to honor at least what little remains of an attempted great liberator leads us to the last item on what may be a historically illusive list of his life: the search for Denmark Vesey's grave.

BLAKE'S LANDS, where according to city authorities Vesey was hanged and, presumably, buried, is no longer identified by this name on twentieth-century maps of Charleston. This former marshland, the possible location of Vesey's gravesite, currently comprises the area between Interstate 26 and the empty dry docks of the now-closed Charleston U.S. Naval Base. Although it has a history of European settlement since the 1700s, this upper section of the peninsula is the industrial, "nonhistoric" district of the city. One approaches what was Blake's Lands by driving northward on Meeting Street away from the antebellum mansions at the Battery and passing underneath the I-26 bridge into the meaner neighborhood of Line Street.

Line Street is the demarcation between the races in modern Charleston. The street also is the namesake and residuum of the earthworks at The Lines, where twenty-two of Vesey's companions were hanged in a single morning in 1822. Today, southward of the intersection of Meeting Street and Line, the population of the city is predominantly white; northward, toward the old Blake's Lands, the residents are predominantly black. There are no historical markers for the 1822 executions. Line Street itself is a struggling row of minority businesses, fast-food restaurants, and sagging frame buildings, where groups of black pedestrians wait at curbsides for city buses that seem perennially late. A white male in an old pickup truck quickly attracts the pedestrians' stares, but more from curiosity than hostility. I appear to be neither a lost tourist nor an addicted suburbanite seeking drugs. The light changes, and I accelerate on Meeting Street, driving past Line Street and toward Vesey's possible burial site.

Blake's Lands have been drained and turned into an industrial site. The area is still only a few feet above sea level. Concealed by the blocks of brick warehouses visible from North Meeting

Street are the city's commercial docks at the west bank of the Cooper River. Farther upstream is the permanently closed U.S. Naval Base. In the better economic times of the Cold War, this facility served the crews of nuclear submarines stationed at Charleston, and these blocks of Meeting Street are still the location of a noticeably large number of "adult" bars. The landmarks from the early nineteenth century—the large tidal marshes and the isolated stand of oak trees where Vesey and his five companions were said to have been hanged—have long since been obliterated by asphalt, neon signs, and railroad tracks.

If Denmark Vesey was executed on Blake's Lands, as the city authorities maintained, it is possible that his body is buried somewhere in this present industrial and economically depressed area. The hangman at the July 2 executions, M. P. Belknap, knew the answer, but he chose not to specify. In a petition to the state legislature, the only primary document extant about the disposal of Vesey's body, Belknap complained, in December 1822, about its slow payment for his services in overseeing Vesey's hanging the previous July, including "the digging of the graves and the various other offices connected with the execution." Belknap's reference to "graves" indicates at least that there is, or was, a gravesite. Apparently, the bodies of Vesey and his five companions were not just summarily thrown into the Cooper River, or taken into Charleston Harbor and then tossed overboard. Belknap did not specify further about the sites of the graves he had dug, or even if the executions had occurred at Blake's Lands. But if Vesey in fact was buried here in an unmarked grave, two centuries of the Cooper River's tidal flooding and the city's industrialization have shifted his final resting place beyond any retrieval.

But in the hope of a historical commemoration of Vesey, I continue to seek the knowledge, or at least the approximate knowledge, of where Vesey was buried. Such an apprehension of historical truth may be contained in the oral insistence by

Charleston's black community that Vesey was hanged not at Blake's Lands but at the Ashley Avenue Oak, and his body buried nearby.

Ashley Avenue runs north-south for several miles in an almost perfectly straight line from Bull Street, where Vesey had his shop and home, to the campus of the Citadel, the military academy founded in response to Vesey's attempted revolt. The twentieth century has been kinder to this neighborhood than to the former Blake's Lands. Bull Street is still a preferred address within the historic district of Charleston, just as it was when Governor Bennett and Denmark Vesey both resided here in 1822; the antebellum mansions of the avenue have since become a major tourist attraction, with horse-drawn carriage tours provided by commercial drivers in ersatz Confederate uniforms.

The spot formerly occupied by the Ashley Avenue Oak is not a scheduled stop on any tours, nor are there any historical plaques identifying this location as the possible site of Vesey's execution in 1822. The site itself is a barely remarkable traffic median on Ashley Avenue, landscaped with a smaller tree to replace the oak cut down in the 1970s. It is located, appropriately, a few blocks north of the intersection of Ashley Avenue and Line Street, toward the "black" side of Line.

If Vesey was in fact hanged here, slightly north of The Lines, where would executioner Belknap have carted the bodies and dug the graves? A logical and practical solution was less than two city blocks to the south, at the Potter's Field, also located on Ashley Avenue. In 1807, the city of Charleston had purchased the unused land on Ashley Avenue between Bee and Doughty streets as a cemetery for the burial of the unknown and indigent dead. This area is clearly marked as "Potters Field" on a Charleston map engraved circa 1820. If Belknap and his helpers had wished in 1822 to dig a grave for Vesey's body that would neither leave any signs for future commemorations by blacks nor be particularly time-consuming for the white executioners, the shallow and unmarked rows of gravesites available at Potter's Field were expediently nearby.

But, as with Blake's Lands, this plot near the center of the city has changed in use during two centuries, with its origins as a cemetery either forgotten or intentionally ignored. Some ten years after Vesey's execution, about 1832, the city sold the tract of land containing Potter's Field. Consequently, this land was used as the site for a U.S. arsenal, a Confederate arsenal, and, by the mid-twentieth century, a private preparatory school for the children of white Charlestonians. No particular care was made to record or exhume the individuals buried there. In 1961, the state of South Carolina purchased the land in order to enlarge the state medical college at Charleston. During the excavations for new buildings in 1963, several human bones, otherwise unidentifiable, were brought to the surface.

The site is now the location for a major teaching hospital. Included in the buildings constructed over the former Potter's Field in the early 1960s was the South Carolina Medical College Hospital, the destination of the civil rights marches led by Coretta Scott King and others in 1968. Hence, when the shouts of "Remember Denmark Vesey!" were raised in these streets three decades ago, both protesters and police may have unwittingly stood a few feet from Vesey's unknown gravesite.

THERE IS A FINAL ITEM on the Spartacus's List of Denmark Vesey's life and death. His burial site may be an industrial wasteland, or an anonymous university building, and the area where grew the oak tree from which he may have been hanged exists only as a traffic median anticlimactically landscaped in the late twentieth century; but the Charleston site where Vesey spent his final hours before his execution—the location of the Work House—is unchanged in its character and racial population. The

Work House and the city's jail for whites once faced each other across a segregated grassy field at Magazine Street. The abandoned three-story building of the former jail still stands, but the Work House was leveled by a major earthquake in 1886 and never reconstructed. On a hot summer day in 1996, I leave behind the flow of tourists on Meeting Street and walk four blocks down Horlbeck's Alley into the unfashionable neighborhood of Magazine Street to see what remains at the site of Vesey's imprisonment.

Where the Work House once stood on Magazine Street is now the location of Robert Mills Manor, a predominantly black public housing project dating from the 1930s. The grassy field formerly separating the Work House from the jail for whites is a parking lot for project residents. Here, in 1769, two black domestics recorded in history only as Dolly and Liverpoole were "burnt on the Work-house Green" on suspicion of having poisoned a white child. The nineteenth-century Charlestonian whose name was given to this housing project, Robert Mills, was a slave-owning architect and the designer of the Washington Monument—that white obelisk that still dominates the capital's skyline. Mills also was the architect for the surviving old jail, and this Gothic building equally dominates the rows of one-story public apartments in front of it. After Mills completed construction of the jail in March 1822, well-traveled Charlestonians compared its architecture to that of London's infamous Newgate Prison. The jail's crenellations and its gray dripstones must have been among the first sights in the city witnessed by Vesey when he was taken from his cell and led to his execution on the morning of July 2.

On a summer afternoon more than a century and a half later, the gaping door at the old jail is hanging open—this historic building is unoccupied, unguarded, and, most remarkably, unmolested by vandals. I walk in the bright sunlight across the parking lot toward the housing project.

The hot and sticky asphalt covering the former Work House green in front of Robert Mills Manor is littered with shards of broken beer bottles. Moving through the shimmering heat waves reflecting off the parking lot's surface of bitumen, I slowly and deliberately step around each spray of broken glass. Two locked and unoccupied city police cars are parked at a sharp V-shaped angle at the farthest end of the lot. At least two Charleston police officers have answered a call from inside the apartments. I am acutely aware that to any black observers I appear as an out-of-place white male, unaccustomedly walking through a black neighborhood, sweating into his white dress shirt and necktie. I decide to limit my walking around the project to an area within sight of the two police cars.

To most white observers unaware of its history, the site of Vesey's former imprisonment might exhibit the Catfish Row quaintness of a stage setting out of *Porgy and Bess*—bright primary colors of laundry hanging on lines strung between apartments at Robert Mills Manor, and a group of laughing female residents, mostly large and maternal-looking, sitting outside in lawn chairs and watching their small children play. The women are seemingly unaware of my presence or of the two police cars. Only close-up, however, does one see the decrepitude of this Depression-era public housing, the evidence of its violence and crime, or the fact that these twentieth-century black residents are as economically imprisoned as Denmark Vesey once was physically imprisoned at the Work House.

There are no architectural remnants of the Work House at this address, nor could Vesey have imagined from his cell the urban landscape of the twentieth-century Robert Mills Manor. His hopes and much of the historical or biographical knowledge of him and the others condemned here at Magazine Street were fated to disappear within the illusory history of a Spartacus's List. The only biographical detail of his imprisonment recorded within the *Official Report* is that, according to his judges, when

Vesey received his sentence of death upstairs at the Work House, silently "the tears trickled down his cheeks."

The time is now late afternoon, a few hours before sunset. As I walk away from Magazine Street, one of the small black children playing outside the apartments, a boy about five or six years of age, suddenly is pushed down by his playmates. He cries loudly, but more from outraged pride than from any pain. As I turn down Horlbeck's Alley, I hear across the parking lot from the housing project a low, rich female laughter—and a question both deeply mocking and deeply loving—from one of the black women sitting in lawn chairs:

"Oh, did they make you cry?"

It is my last impression of Denmark Vesey's life and imprisonment. I rejoin the flow of tourists along Meeting Street, among whom Vesey's life is largely unknown. I answer silently to myself:

Yes, ma'am, they did. They did indeed.

APPENDIX

———◦◦◦◦———

The List Of Those Who Died With Denmark Vesey, 1822

Anderson, Smart. Arrested on July 10. Anderson was a drayman, a driver of a small cart for heavy loads. He attended meetings at Vesey's house and the Bulkley Farm as early as April, and he declared his loyalty to the uprising "to be as much in it as possible." He later stole two muskets, which he concealed on his cart, keeping one for himself and giving the other to a fellow insurrectionist. Anderson was a member of the A.M.E. Church, and he enjoyed calling Monday Gell and his wife "Pa" and "Ma." Hanged on July 26.

Bennett, Batteau. Arrested on June 18. Although "not a principal leader," according to testimony, Bennett "was yet an officer" in Vesey's planned army. On the night of the rebellion, he was "to march with Vesey" to the center of the city. Bennett probably was the recruiter of two adolescents, a free mulatto and a free black. They said they refused him, but were later overheard boasting in the streets that the city's powder magazines were to be exploded and all the whites killed. Arrested, whipped, and released, these two later testified against Bennett in court anonymously as "Witness No. 3" and "Witness No. 4." (Their names were Samuel Guifford and Robert Hadden.) Governor Thomas Bennett formally petitioned the court to spare Batteau Bennett's life, as the conviction was based only upon the testimony of two minors who may have been hoping to avoid further punishment, and because the death of a household slave would cause Governor Bennett "a severe and distressing loss." The request for mercy was denied. Hanged on July 2.

Bennett, Ned. Arrested on June 18. Ned Bennett was characterized by the court as a "man of firm nerves, and desperate courage." Governor Bennett described his slave as "a confidential servant, and his general good conduct was commendable." His judges considered otherwise: "From his looks it was impossible to discover or conjecture what were his feelings." On the night of the revolt, Ned Bennett had hoped to seize the State Arsenal at the Charleston Neck and distribute "between two and three hundred muskets and bayonets, and a few swords." A member of the A.M.E. church, he was among Vesey's original recruits. Hanged on July 2.

Bennett, Rolla. Arrested on June 18. Five defense witnesses testified on Rolla Bennett's behalf, but their testimonies were not recorded by the court. More convincing to his judges were the anonymous claims by two blacks that they had overheard the governor's household slave boast that "my army will first fix my old buck [Governor Bennett] and then the Intendant." Bennett was said throughout his trial to exhibit "uncommon self-possession." He may have been one of the two convicted who "laughed aloud" when taken from their cells on the morning of execution. Hanged on July 2.

Billings, Charles. Arrested on July 18. "Ready and willing" was Billings's response when invited by Vesey and Monday Gell to join in the insurrection. Billings labored at his master's commercial stables, and invited conspirators chosen as horsemen to gather there on the night of the revolt. Hanged on July 26.

Blackwood, Jesse. Arrested on June 23. Blackwood initially was fiercely dedicated to the insurrection. His niece, Sally Howard, testified that he told her "if there were but five men like him they would destroy the city." Blackwood's spouse was the property of another white family; he "had a wife at Mrs. Warings." The pious white widow Mary Beach wrote that Blackwood was "a young creature, only about twenty two," and that "he had a most prepossessing countenance, and *I have* heard that James Legaré [one of the city's judges] wished him pardoned." Visited by a white minister on the morning of his execution, Blackwood stated that "his mind was placid and calm," and that "he was prepared to meet his God." Hanged on July 2.

Clement, Jemmy. Arrested on July 18. Clement also was separated from his wife by slavery. She was the property of "Mrs. Moore's, in St. Thomas Parish." He recruited at least two other insurrectionists from the rural area where his wife was a slave. Clement was a member of the A.M.E. church. Hanged on July 26.

Cohen, Jerry. Arrested on July 19. Cohen was one of the last six participants of the plot to be arrested. He had stated to other conspirators, probably after Vesey's execution on July 2, that "still he was willing to go on, if we went on." Hanged on July 26.

Faber, Polydore. Arrested on July 11. Faber could speak the Gullah language, and he was a member of the A.M.E. church. He was also an acquaintance of "Gullah Jack" Pritchard. Faber was convicted of hiding at least twenty "pike poles" at the Bulkley Farm, to be fitted with blades and used as weapons the night of the insurrection. Hanged on July 26.

Forrest, Julius. Arrested on July 8. Together with his friend and fellow slave Harry Haig, Forrest considered himself to have been "charmed" by "Gullah Jack" Pritchard into joining the insurrection. Forrest spoke openly of his joining Vesey's conspiracy only to one black woman, Prudence Bussacre, who his owner testified "is like a kind of mother to Julius, having raised or brought him up." Prudence Bussacre testified against Forrest at his trial. Hanged on July 26.

Forrester, Lot. Arrested on June 24. Forrester was among Vesey's most active and skilled recruits. He was apparently hired out by his master to a Mr. Peigne, an employee of the State Arsenal. There, Forrester was able to steal a length of "slow match," or fuse, to use in setting fires and explosions throughout the city on the night of the revolt. He stated to Jesse Blackwood that "nothing could be done without fire." Forrester was dispatched by Vesey to gather recruits "up the Santee," indicating a linguistic or other connection to the French Negroes living in concentrations there. Forrester had been a member of the A.M.E. church but had been "turned out" by that congregation for undisclosed reasons sometime prior to the planned revolt. At times, he testified against other conspirators. Hanged on July 26.

Garner, William. Arrested on August 2. Garner was the last of all the Vesey conspirators to be arrested, and the last to be executed. He was probably hired out by his mistress to work as a drayman, and he promised Vesey to lead a company of horsemen on the night of the revolt. He was a member of the A.M.E. church. Garner possessed a pass, signed by his mistress, to travel unaccompanied by whites, presumably for use in his search for work. After the discovery of Vesey's plot, Garner used his pass to escape Charleston, but he was arrested near the state capital of Columbia. During his trial, Garner made a half-hour speech in his own defense, which, according to his Charleston judges, "would have done honor to an educated man." Hanged on August 9, by which date Vesey had hoped to have brought his followers toward their permanent freedom in Africa.

Glenn, Jack. Arrested on July 16. Glenn was lame in both feet, but he told Vesey that he would willingly serve as a horseman in the battle on the night of the revolt. At a meeting at Vesey's house where Polydore Faber and "Gullah Jack" Pritchard had discussed obtaining edged weapons, Glenn haltingly walked and "carried about a hat to get money to pay a man to make pikes." He was a member of the A.M.E. church. Hanged on July 26.

Hammett, Bacchus. Arrested on July 11. In April and May of 1822, Hammett had been an eager participant in meetings at Vesey's shop and the Bulkley farm, and he later took a pistol, a sword, and a keg of gunpowder to Vesey's house. Hammett, by his own description, "was the Devil amongst women." On his procession to the gallows he shocked white spectators by "laughing and bidding his acquaintances in the streets 'good bye.'" His actions were interpreted by whites as his being reduced to a state of idiocy by fear. (In 1718, the captured pirate Stede Bonnet had been hanged at Charleston, having traveled to his gallows clutching a bouquet of wildflowers and waving gaily to the crowds. This incident with a white man was remembered in the city as a fine example of English nerve.) At the scaffold, the mechanism failed, and Hammett did not drop. Then, in the astonished words of one witness, Bacchus Hammett *threw himself forward, and as he swung back he lifted his feet, so that his knees might not touch the Board!* Hammett probably was the conspirator reported as being shot with a pistol by Captain Dove of the city watch while he still dangled alive from the rope, an act more of outrage than mercy. Hanged on July 26.

Harth, Mingo. Arrested on June 21. As a slave, Harth was classified as a "mechanic," meaning he was either a skilled or semiskilled laborer. By birth, he was an African, a Mandingo. He was an acquaintance of "Gullah Jack" Pritchard, but for either cultural or personal reasons, he chose to serve under Peter Poyas's command. Harth was a major recruiter for Vesey both among the city's black Methodists and at the lumberyard owned by his master. Harth would visit "at his wife's house," indicating that she was owned by another master. It was to Mingo Harth's quarters that William Paul, one of the original betrayers of the plot, went to study the Bible and decide whether to inform. Paul consequently testified against Harth during the latter's trial. Hanged on July 26.

Horry, John. Arrested on July 5. Horry was a coachman, had a sword, and intended to use it on his master—"to rip open your belly," he told the astonished Elias Horry. Hanged alongside of "Gullah Jack" Pritchard on July 12.

Jore, Joe. Arrested on July 6. Jore was an African, an Ibo, and also had acquaintances or relatives among the French Negroes. There is no record of his A.M.E. membership, but he probably was acquainted with the Reverend Morris Brown. Jore previously had worked as a cook for Colonel Cross, the attorney of record for Denmark Vesey. Other blacks considered him an invalid, but Jore promised to take a sword and fight on the night of the rebellion. Hanged on July 26.

McNeil, Jack. Arrested on July 22. McNeil was sold into slavery at Charleston when he was a boy "about seven years of age," having been taken by a slave ship from Africa. As this transaction could have occurred legally no later than 1807, McNeil was approximately in his early twenties when he was executed. He was a member of the A.M.E. church. Hanged on July 30.

Mitchell, Dean. Arrested on July 19. Mitchell had known early about the Vesey plot, and he stated that "he saw the thing was going on well, and he was glad of it." He assisted "Gullah Jack" Pritchard and Jack Glenn in collecting money to make spears or pikes. Mitchell was a member of the A.M.E. church. Hanged on July 26.

Poyas, Peter. Arrested on June 18. "Intrepid and resolute" was the characterization of Poyas even by his white judges. Poyas was one of the three conspirators—the others were Vesey and Gell—known to have been able to write "in a good hand." He probably recorded many of the secret lists of Vesey's recruits. Poyas labored as a ship's carpenter. Questioned one day on the street by Ned Bennett about the firmness of his commitment to the revolt, Poyas turned to a nearby tree planted in a box and struck the wood with his hand, exclaiming he was "firm as this box." Rolla Bennett, even after his conviction, claimed he "never conversed" with Poyas, perhaps an attempt to save the latter's life. Poyas was a member of the A.M.E. church. He may have been one of the two who laughed aloud at their captors when the condemned were taken from their cells on the morning of their execution. Hanged on July 2.

Pritchard, "Gullah Jack." Arrested on July 5. Pritchard was a diminutive man, whose small hands and frame rendered him unsuitable for field work, but he made himself useful as a general-purpose laborer and dockside messenger at his master's shipyard. His reputation as a "conjure man" among both blacks and whites also may have added to his value as a property. To his master, Pritchard perhaps was recognized as an inexpensive source of naturopathic medicines for other ailing slaves. Pritchard reputedly could concoct occult poisons as well as medicines, and this rumored ability made him second only to Vesey as the most-feared among the conspirators. The city judges intentionally deleted from the *Official Report* the testimonies by other slaves that Pritchard intended to poison the wells and pumps of white families in the days preceding Vesey's revolt. (Intentional poisoning by blacks was a constant anxiety among whites in Charleston, where black domestics prepared the meals, nursed the sick, and tended the newborn.) Pritchard was an African, an Angolan, and a sometime attendant at the A.M.E. church. His access to a canoe made him particularly valuable to Vesey as a recruiter among the coastal Gullah people and the riverine French Negroes. After his sentencing, Pritchard asked for a two-week stay of execution in order to compose himself by the use of Christian and Obeah rituals. This request was denied. The court accused Pritchard of having "endeavored to enlist on your behalf all the powers of darkness, and employed for that purpose the most disgusting mummery and superstition." Hanged on July 12.

Purcell, Jack. Arrested on July 12. Purcell was among Vesey's first recruits, and one of the few mulattoes chosen to participate in the plot. At the gallows, Purcell lamented that "if it had not been for the cunning of that old villain, Vesey, I should not now be in my present situation." Hanged on July 26.

Robertson, Adam. Arrested on July 11. Robertson was a member of Jack Pritchard's Gullah Company, and he was present at the meeting at the Bulkley Farm where a fowl was half-roasted and eaten still bloody by all members of the company as a sign of their union. He was also a member of the A.M.E. church. Hanged on July 26.

Robertson, John. Arrested on July 11. Robertson also was a member of the Gullah Company and the A.M.E. church. It was a possible indignity to him that his white master, also named John Robertson, had given him the same first name—an act of misplaced affection, attempted dominance, or indifference. Hanged on July 26.

Robertson, Robert. Arrested on July 11. Robertson helped "Gullah Jack" Pritchard and Tom Russel conceal pikes and spears for use by the Gullah Company and the French Negroes. At the meeting at the Bulkley Farm, he brought a pistol, which he presumably had success-fully stolen from his master. He was the only conspirator from the Robertson farm for which there is no documentation of A.M.E. membership. Hanged on July 26.

Russel, Tom. Arrested on July 10. Russel was a blacksmith, and probably was the skilled slave whom Vesey did not identify to other conspirators, who was willing to forge pikeheads and spearheads for the conspiracy if the recruits took up a collection "to pay that black man's wages to his mistress." Tom Russel was owned by a Mrs. Russel and probably was hired out for wages payable to her. Russel was fluent in Gullah, and often spoke with Jack Pritchard in that language. In addition to his smithy work, Russel was said to have been trained by Pritchard to be his partner as an Obeah-man, or master of sympathetic magic. Pritchard later advised members of the Gullah Company that "when you don't see me, and see Tom, you see me." Hanged on July 26, fourteen days after the death of Pritchard.

Scott, Tom. Arrested on July 24. Scott was a member of Monday Gell's company, and, therefore, possibly an African Ibo. Scott was separated from his wife by slavery; she was the property of Mingo Harth's master. He was a member of the A.M.E. church. Hanged on July 30.

Simms, Dick. Arrested on July 13. Simms was the property of a notably literary and melancholic Charleston family. His master, William Simms, once advised his son, a novelist, to avoid Charleston, "as a place of *tombs*." Dick Simms was a member of the Gullah Company, and may also have stolen a pistol to take to the Bulkley Farm. Simms was defended vigorously by his master at the trials, and William Simms's pointed cross-examinations of hostile witnesses were among the few such exchanges recorded in the *Official Report*. Despite his master's efforts, the defense for Dick Simms was unsuccessful. Hanged on July 26.

Smith, Caesar. Arrested on July 22. Smith was an African and a member of Gell's Ibo Company. He labored as a drayman and was probably hired out for his wages by his owner, a Miss Smith. He possessed a sword, obtained for him by Vesey, and was a member of the A.M.E. church. Hanged on July 30.

Stagg, Jacob. Arrested on July 23. Stagg, a mulatto, was hired out by his master as a housepainter, and he told other members of the conspiracy that "he was tired of paying wages" to his master. Stagg had a wife who was the property of another master, Dr. David Ramsey, a member of the Independent Congregational Circular Church. Stagg's master assured the court that his slave "was always home at night." Monday Gell was unable to obtain a sword for Stagg, but the housepainter replied that he "would get a scythe and make a sword out of it" for use on the night of the rebellion. Hanged on July 30.

Thompson, Pharo. Arrested on July 13. Stagg's idea for a weapon may have been suggested to him by Thompson, his fellow mulatto, who possessed a sword fashioned from a scythe. This weapon probably was made for Thompson by the blacksmith and Obeah-man, Tom Russel. Monday Gell testified that on Sunday, June 16, the date originally set by Vesey for the revolution, Thompson pointed "to the Archdale Church, where the white people are," and lamented to Gell, "When will we be like them?" After the arrest of Peter Poyas, Thompson asserted that if he could only obtain a pass signed by his master and a fifty-dollar bill, he would "take his horse and run away" northward to freedom. His plan was unsuccessful. Thompson was defended at his trial by Dr. Ramsey, the owner of Jacob Stagg's wife. Hanged on July 26.

Yates, Adam. Arrested on July 18. Yates was given the responsibility by Vesey of making certain that the rural blacks on the night of the revolt came down the Charleston Neck at the city peninsula and resisted any white reinforcements arriving from farther inland. He had a long knife, or bayonet, "such as the one riflemen wear." Hanged on July 26.

Yates, Bellisle. Arrested on July 18. Yates was responsible for hiding plantation blacks in the yards of Charleston households on the night of June 16, when they would join the urban slaves in revolt. He was a member of the A.M.E. church. Hanged on July 26.

Yates, Naphur. Arrested on July 18. Yates attended Vesey's meetings at the Bulkley Farm, where he and Adam Yates raised their hands and swore "their hearts were in this business." Naphur Yates may have taken biblical instruction by Vesey on the unusual significance of his slave-given first name: In II Maccabees 1:36, the word *naphur* is identified as the "purification fire" of the Israelite slaves, with which they would destroy their masters. Hanged on July 26.

THE BIOGRAPHICAL INFORMATION in this appendix was gathered from the *Official Report*, U.S. census reports, manuscript confessions, or private correspondence. The slave epitaphs remain only in information that their masters wished to be recorded.

Four white men—described by Charleston's judges as a Scottish privateer, a Spanish sailor, a German peddler, and a "well known" local confidence man—were jailed and fined in late 1822 for having spoken favorably to city blacks about Denmark Vesey or his coconspirators. Particularly infuriating to the city judges was the question posed by the Spanish sailor publicly to Charleston's slaves: "If you had a favor to ask, would you ask it of a white man or a black man?"

Of the total of 131 blacks and mulattoes arrested in the Vesey plot, fifteen were acquitted and thirty-eight were discharged after imprisonment or whippings at the Work House. Among those whipped was Peter Cooper, described by his judges during his trial as "an elderly Negro man." He received twenty lashes. Forty-three other conspirators were sentenced to be "transported"—sent at their owner's expense into slavery outside the state, usually at plantations farther south in Georgia, Alabama, or Mississippi.

Charles Drayton, John Enslow, Frank Ferguson, Monday Gell, and Peirault Strohecker testified against some or all of the thirty-four condemned men listed above. These five slaves were allowed to live.

ACKNOWLEDGMENTS

For the past ten years, my literary work has rewarded me with two published biographies, one published novel, a few poems, and an even score of good friends. I consider myself richer than most writers, for the editor and the literary agent of this biography have shown themselves to be among that number of friends. Ashbel Green, my editor at Knopf, and John Ware, my literary agent, I hereby thank publicly for their goodwill demonstrated toward me and my writing.

Kurt Neiburg, Vick Neapolitan, and Rebecca Scott each provided a "room of one's own" when it was most needed in order to complete this book. Karen Swann, of TypeRight, at Clemson, South Carolina, typed the words, extended credit, and provided me with invaluable advice from that most valued of readers, the educated layperson.

Three published books and six named friends are not a bad tally for a decade, particularly for one's difficult fifties. I entertain hopes that I shall have at least three more books and six more friends to offer gratefully to the public in the future.

Guilford Walpole, of St. John's Island, South Carolina, and the staff at the South Carolina Historical Society also greatly aided me in my research. Theirs is the credit if this biography finds historical validity; mine is the fault if it contains factual error.

NOTES

———◆◆◆———

Throughout the notes that follow, the sources listed below are cited only in the abbreviated forms shown.

Beach correspondence: Letters written regarding the Vesey conspiracy during the summer of 1822 by Mary Lamboll Beach of Charleston to her sister Elizabeth Lamboll Thomas of Philadelphia. This correspondence is published here for the first time. The originals are preserved at the SCHS, retrievable under archival accession number 43-225.

Official Report: Lionel H. Kennedy and Thomas Parker, eds., *An Official Report of the Trials of Sundry Negroes Charged with an Attempt to Raise an Insurrection in the State of South Carolina: Preceded by an Introduction and Narrative* (James R. Schenck, Charleston, 1822). Cited pagination is to the archival reprint by Beacon Press, 1970.

SCDAH: South Carolina Department of Archives and History, Columbia, South Carolina.

SCHS: South Carolina Historical Society, Charleston, South Carolina.

INTRODUCTION: THE REALITY OF DENMARK VESEY

PAGE

3-4 *"If black leaders"* to *"a liberator whom God sent": Charleston* (SC) *News and Courier,* 10 August 1976, B1; 11 August 1976, A8:3.

5 *withheld diplomatic recognition:* Rayford W. Logan, *The Diplomatic Relations of the United States with Haiti 1796–1891* (UNC Press, 1941), 200–201, 303.

saw in the events at Charleston: William Johnson to Thomas Jefferson, 10 December 1822, cited in Donald G. Morgan, *Justice William Johnson: The First Dissenter* (USC Press, 1954), 138.

"The Star-Spangled Banner": Joel Williamson, *After Slavery: The Negro in South Carolina During Reconstruction* (UNC Press, 1965), 258–259.

Denmark Vesey's son: Charleston (SC) *Daily Courier,* 15 April 1865.

6 *"he remained immovable"* to *"Die silent, as you shall see me do": Official Report,* 30, 15, 31.

"docile slave into a revolutionary": Joseph Furnas, *The Road to Harpers Ferry* (William Sloane Associates, 1959), 419.

7 *"dangerous document for slaves": Official Report,* xxii.

7–8 *"At the head of the conspiracy"* to *"he had not a will": Official Report,* "Narrative," 1; "Extracts," 160–161; "Confession of Jack Purcell," 88; "Evidence of Frank Ferguson," 63.

8 *"peculiar reality":* William W. Freehling, "Denmark Vesey's Peculiar Reality," in *New Perspectives on Race and Slavery in America,* eds. Robert Abzug and Stephen Maizlish (University of KY Press, 1986), 43–44.

9 *first name is alien:* The Kingdom of Denmark proscribed the importation of slaves, but not slavery, among its colonies in 1792. See "The Danish West Indies," in Glyn Jones, *Denmark* (Praeger, 1970), 244.

10 *"he did not associate"* to *"there was but one Minister": Official Report,* "The Trials," 135; "Trial of William Palmer," 112.

I. THE MEN FROM BARBADOS

11 *a black slave:* Peter H. Wood, *Black Majority: Negroes in Colonial South Carolina from 1670 Through the Stono Rebellion* (Knopf, 1974), 20–21. Walter J. Fraser, Jr., *Charleston! Charleston! The History of a Southern City* (USC Press, 1989), 1–4.

12 *roughly one in four:* Robert Higgins, "Charleston: Terminus and Entrepôt of the Colonial Slave Trade," in *The African Diaspora:*

Interpretive Essays, ed. Martin Kilson et al. (Harvard University Press, 1976), 118; Wood, *Black Majority*, xiv.

12 *"sixpence throwne down"* to *a planter elite:* Richard G. Dunn, *Sugar and Slaves: The Rise of the Planter Class in the English West Indies, 1624–1713* (UNC Press, 1972), 5, 20, 46, 58.

13 *two ruling classes:* J. P. Thomas, Jr., "The Barbadians in Early South Carolina," *South Carolina Historical and Genealogical Magazine* 31 (April 1930): 89–91.

13–15 *"Carolina in ye West Indies"* to *"He has brought negroes and expects more":* T. Modyford and P. Colleton to Proprietors, 12 August 1663, SCHS; Locke quoted in Wood, *Black Majority*, 18–20, 23, 33.

15 *enslaving more Indians:* John Duncan, "Servitude and Slavery in Colonial South Carolina, 1670–1776" (Ph.D. diss., 1972, Emory University), 1; Amy Friedlander, "Indian Slavery in Proprietary South Carolina" (MA thesis, 1975, Emory University), 4; Eugene Sirmans, *Colonial South Carolina: A Political History 1663–1763* (UNC Press, 1966), 24–25.

"The Barbadians endeavor to rule all": Locke quoted in Wood, *Black Majority*, 24.

16 *cosmopolitan in its slavery:* Fraser, *Charleston*, 63–64, 111, 121, 130–131, 179. The Charleston slavers used a variety of terms in their shipping manifests and newspaper advertisements, such as *Ibo* and *Coramantee*, which are difficult to correlate with present-day African national boundaries and linguistic groups. Michael Mullin, in *Africa in America: Slave Acculturation and Resistance in the American South and the British Caribbean, 1736–1831* (University of IL Press, 1992), 282–283, provides a useful correlation between eighteenth- and nineteenth-century terminology used by white slavers and the twentieth-century location of where in Africa these black people may have come from. See also the map and accompanying discussion in Daniel C. Littlefield, *Rice and Slaves: Ethnicity and the Slave Trade in Colonial South Carolina* (LSU Press, 1981), 21–23.

17 *copied almost word for word:* Fraser, *Charleston*, 15, 67; Dunn, *Sugar and Slaves*, 239–240.

18 *a black majority:* Richard Dunn, "The English Sugar Islands and the Founding of South Carolina," *South Carolina Historical Magazine*

72 (April 1971): 92–93; Wood, *Black Majority,* 131; Fraser, *Charleston,* 28, 42, 135.

18 *"looks more like a negro country":* "Samuel Dyssli to His Mother, Brothers, and Friends in Switzerland, December 3, 1737," reprinted in *South Carolina Historical and Genealogical Magazine* 23 (July 1922): 89–90.

19 *"I cannot to this day":* Frank J. Klingberg, ed., *The Carolina Chronicles of Dr. Francis Le Jau 1706–1717* (University of CA Press, 1956), 22, 52, 102.

"the grandest hall" to *"great fear":* "Journal of Josiah Quincy, Junior, 1773," reprinted in *Proceedings of the Massachusetts Historical Society* 49 (June 1916): 441–456.

20 *"appeal of Venice":* George C. Rogers, Jr., *Charleston in the Age of the Pinckneys* (University of OK Press, 1969), 63.

"Flame and Power" to *"crying Voice":* Quoted from contemporaneous descriptions in David T. Morgan, "The Great Awakening in South Carolina 1740–1775," *South Atlantic Quarterly* 70, 4 (1971): 597, 600.

20-1 *"abuse and cruelty"* to *"all good men":* George Whitefield, "A Letter to the Inhabitants of Maryland, Virginia, North and South-Carolina," reprinted in *The Works of the Reverend George Whitefield* (London, 1771), vol. 4, 37–41.

21 *"Who can bring"* to *"Bathe my soul":* John Conder and Thomas Gibbons, eds., *Living Christianity Delineated, in the Diaries and Letters of Two Eminently Pious Persons Lately Deceased: by Mr. Hugh Bryan and Mrs. Mary Hutson* (Boston, 1809), 6, 9, 54–55.

"great Assemblies of Negroes": "Wednesday, the 17th day of February, 1742," *Colonial Records of South Carolina: The Journal of the Commons House of Assembly* (USC Press, 1951–1962), vol. 3, 381–382. Hereafter cited as *SC Commons Journal.*

21-2 *"a Moorish slave woman"* to *"many Days' intimate":* Quoted from contemporaneous sources in Leigh Schmidt, "'The Grand Prophet,' Hugh Bryan: Early Evangelism's Challenge to the Establishment and Slavery in the Colonial South," *South Carolina Historical Magazine* 87 (October 1986): 242–243, 248.

22 *"Destruction of Charles Town":* SC Commons Journal,* vol. 4, 72.

22 *"The cry is Repent":* Conder and Gibbons, eds., *Living Christianity Delineated,* 50.

"Delusion of Satan": SC Commons Journal, vol. 3, 461–462.

23–5 *banks of the Stono River* to *"cutt off their heads":* Peter Wood, in *Black Majority,* was the first historian to place the Stono Rebellion within a demographic and economic context, rigorously examining extant primary sources. His account, 314–320, remains definitive.

25 *"This small society of rice and cotton planters":* Henry Adams, *History of the United States of America during the First Administration of Thomas Jefferson* (Charles Scribner's Sons, 1891), 149.

26 *Taverns and other public houses . . . the display of animal oddities:* Fraser, *Charleston,* 115–116, 186. Peter A. Coclanis, in *Shadow of a Dream: Economic Life and Death in the South Carolina Low-Country 1670–1920* (Oxford University Press, 1989), 11, argues that the residential architecture unique to Charleston—the "recoil from the street" of the typical eighteenth-century house of slave owners and "its retreat behind high walls"—signifies the "pathogenic nature" of a transplanted Caribbean police state.

cargo of 104 slaves: Elizabeth Donnan, *Documents Illustrative of the History of the Slave Trade to America* (Carnegie Institute, 1935), "Negroes Imported into South Carolina, 1783," vol. 4, 474.

2. A PLACE CALLED CHARLESTON IN THE CHRISTIAN LANGUAGE

28 *noticeably light-complexioned man:* Records and genealogical research of Mrs. Dewey C. Whitenton, Bolivar, TN. Mrs. Whitenton is the great-great-great-granddaughter of Captain Vesey.

29 *cargo of 390 slaves . . . beauty and intelligence: Official Report,* "Extracts," 160–161.

31 *"spoke French with fluency": Ibid.,* 72.

continued at sea as a slaver: John Lofton, *Insurrection in South Carolina: The Turbulent World of Denmark Vesey* (Antioch Press, 1964), 3.

32 *smell a slave ship:* Walter J. Fraser, Jr., *Charleston, Charleston!: The History of a Southern City* (UNC Press, 1989), 110–111.

33 *black corpses littering:* George C. Rogers, Jr., *Charleston in the Age of the Pinckneys* (University of OK Press, 1956), 27.

head of a household . . . Christ Episcopal Church: Department of Commerce and Labor, Bureau of the Census, *Heads of Families At the First Census of the United States Taken in the Year 1790, South Carolina* (Government Printing Office, 1908), 40; Whitenton records. See also the death notice of Captain Vesey, *Charleston Courier*, 21 May 1835: "The Relatives, Friends, and Acquaintances of Capt. Vesey, also the Friends of Mr. Robert Stuart, and the Officers and Members of the Charleston Marine Society are respectfully invited to attend the Funeral of Capt. Vesey, from the residence of Mr. Robert Stuart, in Black Bird Alley, This Afternoon, at 4 o'clock."

34 *South Carolina sui generis:* The population totals for blacks and whites in Charleston for 1790–1800 differ in the tables for these decades published by W. B. Phillips, "The Slave Labor Problem in the Charleston District," in Eugene Genovese, ed., *The Slave Economy of the Old South: Selected Essays in Economic and Social History* (LSU Press, 1968), 203, and E. Horace Fitchett, "The Origin and Growth of the Free Negro Population of Charleston, South Carolina," *Journal of Negro History* 26 (October 1941): 435. The totals in this biography are for the greater Charleston District, an administrative area recognized by the early U.S. census, comprising parts of present-day Berkeley and Colleton counties, South Carolina. For a map of the greater Charleston District, see Ronald Jackson and David Schaefemeyer, eds., *South Carolina 1820 Census Index*, "South Carolina Counties & Circuit Court Districts, A.D. 1785, Compiled by Historical Records Survey, W.P.A., 1938" (Accelerated Indexing Systems, Inc., 1976), xxiv; the totals are specifically enumerated in "Schedule of the Whole Numbers of Persons in the District of South Carolina," *Second Census of the United States* (Duane, 1801), 2M. See also the totals for these decades for the Charleston District in *The Growth and Distribution of Population in South Carolina* (USC Press, 1943), 71.

All recent historians and enumerators agree, however, on the singularity of South Carolina as the state of a black majority with a continued African identity. In the judgment of one scholar, "the continued heavy importation of slaves until 1808 slowed the [demographic] shift from Africans to Creoles," or to a predominance of black Americans born in South Carolina into second- or third-generation slavery; Peter Kolchin, *American Slavery 1619–1877* (Hill and Wang, 1993), 38. See also W. Robert Higgins, "The Geographical Origin of Negro Slaves in Colonial South Carolina," *South Atlantic Quarterly* 70 (Winter 1971): 47, who says that the majority of black slaves in the southern colonial period came "from Africa directly to Charleston and the lesser ports of South Carolina."

34 *forbidden to appear:* Fraser, *Charleston*, 190.

a loud tattoo: J. S. Buckingham, *The Slave States of America* (London: Fisher, Son, and Company, 1842), 568–569.

35 *arrested by the Guard:* W. H. Wilson, *Reminiscences of William Hasell Wilson (1811–1902)* (Patterson and White Co., 1937), 7–8.

Work House: "Magazine Street," in "Information for Guides of Historical Charleston," unpublished monograph, SCHS, 328–329.

"for a little sugar": Fraser, *Charleston*, 164, 203.

36 *blacks "at their pleasure":* South Carolina Gazette, 20 June 1768.

37 *present in the laboring crowds:* Lofton, *Insurrection in South Carolina*, 68.

expansion of Islam: Michael A. Gorney, "Muslims in Early America," *Journal of Southern History* 40, 4 (November 1994): 677–682, 686–687.

"I knew several": Charles Ball, *Fifty Years in Chains* (Dover, 1970), 164–165.

approximately 8,800: D. Austin, ed., *African Muslims in Antebellum America: A Sourcebook* (Garland, 1984), 35–36.

38 *"a place called Charleston":* "Omar's Autobiography, 1831, Translated," in Austin, ed., *African Muslims in Antebellum America*, 464–466.

39 *Archibald Johnson:* It is possible that Omar Ibn Said's escape was not advertised, with a reward offered for his capture, but these published notices were customary in the Charleston newspapers. Ibn Said does not state his former master's first name in his autobiography, but only one Johnson advertised in the Charleston papers for the return of a runaway slave in 1810, the year of Ibn Said's escape. This Archibald Johnson offered twenty dollars that

year for the return of a slave who matched Ibn Said's age, appearance, and intelligence: "about 31 years of age; 5 feet 7 or 8 inches high. He is a very likely Negro. . . ." This advertisement further refers to the slave as having "formerly belonged to Mr. Ewing's estate at Parker's Ferry. . . ." See *Charleston Courier,* 6 February 1810. This prior ownership matches the personal history written by Ibn Said, in which he tells of his being owned by one master who was tolerably humane, before being sold a second time into "the hand of Johnson."

There is no exact equivalent or transliteration of the name of Omar into the English language. Archibald Johnson advertised his runaway slave as being called Andrew. White masters, particularly in the Africanized low country of South Carolina and Georgia, frequently assigned to their slaves English first names with the same assonance or syllabic stress as the African name by which the black person told his master he had been called. The African name Cudjo, for example, often became Joe in slavery. Hence, the rendering of Omar into Andrew is not unreasonable. See Peter H. Wood, *Black Majority: Negroes in Colonial South Carolina from 1670 Through the Stono Rebellion* (Knopf, 1974), 181–183.

39 *Dorchester:* Lofton, *Insurrection in South Carolina,* 28.

40 *a religious significance:* The Islamic year 1238, reckoned by the lunar calendar, began on September 18, 1822, by the Christian calendar. Calculations by Oriental Division, New York City Public Library, 1997.

one of various sayings: Oxford Encyclopedia of the Modern Islamic World (Oxford University Press, 1995), vol. 2, 83–87.

held the winning lottery ticket: Charleston City Gazette, 9 December 1799; *Official Report,* "Extracts," 161.

3. THE AFRICAN CHURCH AND DENMARK VESEY AS PROPHET

41 *house at 20 Bull Street:* "Methodology Used in Locating Denmark Vesey's House" (unpublished monograph), Avery Research Center for African American History and Culture, College of Charleston, South Carolina.

42 *member of Second Presbyterian Church:* Mrs. Samuel Stoney to Anne Gregory, 21 August 1939, SCHS; Erskine Clarke, *Wrestlin' Jacob: A Portrait of Religion in the Old South* (John Knox Press, 1979), 147. Clarke notes that since Vesey was carried on the Presbyterian church rolls but not recorded as undergoing a baptism at Second Presbyterian, he may have "already been baptized and very well may have been a member of another church," 195—i.e., the A.M.E. church.

$600 of his lottery winnings: Official Report, "Extracts," 161.

average wage of one dollar: Robert Mills, *Statistics of South Carolina* (Hurbert and Lloyd, 1826), 427–428.

43 *taken to court seven times: Consolidated Index of South Carolina, 1695–1925,* South Carolina Department of Archives and History (SCDAH), 32167–32170.

"he was satisfied": Official Report, "Confession of Monday Gell," 70. This quote was repeated in print by the Massachusetts abolitionist, Union officer, and literary acquaintance of Emily Dickinson, Thomas Higginson, in Higginson's biography of Vesey, "Denmark Vesey," reprinted in full in William L. Katz, ed., *Black Rebellion: Selections from Travelers and Outlaws* (Arno Press, 1969), 227.

"looked very much like Denmark": Official Report, "Confession of Bacchus Hammett," 107.

44 *may have been Susan Vesey: State Free Negro Capitation Tax Books, Charleston, South Carolina, 1811–1860, Book Two, 1821–1822,* SCDAH.

Nor was he a mulatto: Vesey's supposed white ancestry, frequently cited by local historians as fact, apparently was first asserted by the nineteenth-century South Carolina novelist and historian William Gilmore Simms, who described Vesey as "a mulatto of great personal beauty," *History of South Carolina* (S. Babcock, 1849), 328.

a little under 6 percent: Robert L. Harris, Jr., "Charleston's Free Afro-American Elite: The Brown Fellowship Society and the Humane Brotherhood," *South Carolina Historical Magazine* 82 (October 1981): 303.

"balls given by Negro": Social observation by the eighteenth-century traveler Ebenezer Hazard, quoted in Walter J. Fraser, Jr.,

Charleston, Charleston!: The History of a Southern City (UNC Press, 1989), 130.

45 *Jehu Jones . . . possessed six slaves:* Larry Koger, *Black Slaveowners: Free Black Slavemasters in South Carolina 1790–1860* (McFarland & Co., 1985), 169, 173; Harris, "Charleston's Free Afro-American Elite," 308.

Brown Fellowship Society: Harris, "Charleston's Free Afro-American Elite," 292–295. Koger, in *Black Slaveowners*, 160–183, argues that Vesey's plot was betrayed because of the economic antagonism and social pride of members of the city's mulatto elite. Whether this elite was in fact recognized as such by the white ruling class of Charleston's police state is open to debate. Eugene D. Genovese has aspersed other southern historians as becoming "entranced with the Brown Fellowship Society," and not recognizing Charleston's closed economic and military slave polis for what it was. See Genovese, "The Slave States of North America," in David W. Cohen and Jack P. Greene, eds., *Neither Slave Nor Free: The Freedmen of African Descent in the Slave Societies of the New World* (Johns Hopkins Press, 1972), 271.

46 *the African church . . . Vesey's move to the congregation:* Marina Wikeramanayake, "The Free Negro in Ante-Bellum South Carolina" (Ph.D. diss., 1966, University of WI), 167–170; *Official Report*, "Narrative," 14.

47–8 *"He studied the Bible"* to *more than he feared God: Official Report*, "Trial of Denmark Vesey, Evidence of William Paul," 61; "Narrative," 11; "Confession of Rolla Bennett," 46; "Narrative," 12.

48 *"acted the fool"* to *"little man":* Ibid., "Narrative," 31–32; "Trial of Peter Poyas, Evidence of Witness No. 5," 52.

49 *intimated to Brown:* An unspoken agenda among the judges at the Vesey trial may have been to complete the destruction of the A.M.E. church and to indict Rev. Morris Brown under the capital offense of insurrection. (See chapters 6 and 7.)

"Almost every night": Charleston Times, 17 July 1816.

50 *"they having bought a lot": Charleston City Gazette and Commercial Advertiser*, 4 December 1817.

correspondent styled "Patriot": Charleston Courier, 9 June 1818.

51 *only "avenue for self-expression":* Wikeramanayake, "The Free Negro in Ante-Bellum South Carolina," 155.

"Gullah people were ready": Official Report, "Confession of Smart Anderson," 89.

52 *"the distressed inhabitants"* to *Captain Joseph Vesey was appointed:* Quoted in John Lofton, *Insurrection in South Carolina: The Turbulent World of Denmark Vesey* (Antioch Press, 1964), 70; James W. Hagy, *People and Professions of Charleston, South Carolina, 1782–1802* (Clearfield Publishers, 1992), 21.

53 *"Every principle which could operate": Official Report,* "Narrative," 13.

54–5 *"all men were born equal"* to *"You deserve to remain slaves":* Ibid., 12.

55 *detention by the state's militia:* H. M. Henry, *The Police Control of the Slave in South Carolina* (Emory and Henry College, 1914), 36–37, 43–45.

"firm nerves" to *"it was impossible": Official Report,* "Narrative," 15, 31.

56 *"uncommon self-possession"* to *"the governor treats":* Ibid., "Narrative," 15, 29; "Trial of Rolla Bennett, Confession," 46.

"enjoyed all the substantial comforts" to *Gell was an African Ibo:* Ibid., "Narrative," 29; "The Trial of Monday Gell," 66.

"a first-rate ship's carpenter" to *"We cannot go on":* Ibid., "Narrative," 16, 22, 29; Higginson, "Denmark Vesey," 229.

4. NOTHING CAN BE DONE WITHOUT FIRE

57 *On a pleasant evening:* The approximate chronology in late May and the specific details of this meeting at Vesey's house were obtained by internal dating and comparisons from among the following sources in *Official Report:* "Trial of Rolla Bennett," 42, 44–46; "Trial of Peter Poyas," 50; "Trial of Denmark Vesey, Testimony of Frank Ferguson," 63; "Trial of Monday Gell," 65–67; "Confession of Monday Gell," 70; "Trial of Gullah Jack," 78; and "Trial of Bacchus Hammett," 109–110.

It must be remembered that each of these confessions or testimonies was obtained under threats of death or torture; but the consistent details in separate testimonies, such as "Mr. Duncan's trees," indicate that some speakers were remarkably well rehearsed, or that this meeting at Vesey's house took place at the approximate date and manner in which it is described in the text.

57 *house was a respectable dwelling:* "Methodology Used in Locating Denmark Vesey's House" (unpublished monograph), Avery Research Center for African American History and Culture, College of Charleston, South Carolina.

59 *"I will show you the man":* *Official Report,* "Trial of Rolla Bennett, Testimony of Witness No. 6," 45; "Trial of Peter Poyas, Testimony of Witness No. 5," 50.

a list of six hundred names: Ibid., "Narrative," 16.

59–60 *"nothing could be done without fire"* to *"when the bells rang":* Ibid., "Trial of Jack Glenn, Testimony of Monday Gell," 98, 46.

60 *in his subsequent plans:* Ibid., "Narrative," 23–26; "Trial of Gullah Jack, Testimony of Witness No. 10," 77.

61 *access to a horse* to *"to ride through the streets":* Ibid., "Narrative," 26.

61–2 *"very skillful in making swords"* to *"to pay that black man's wages":* Ibid., "Trial of William Colock, Testimony of Monday Gell," 95; "Narrative," 23; "Trial of John Vincent, Testimony of Monday Gell," 126; "Narrative," 26–27; "Trial of Bacchus Hammett, Confession," 109–110; "Trial of Jerry Cohen, Testimony of John Enslow," 119–120.

62 *blacks were allowed to congregate:* Ibid., "Narrative," xvi, 27. The "Sunday market" tradition was, interestingly, strongest since the eighteenth century on the Caribbean islands of Vesey's probable birth and adolescence, the Danish Virgin Islands. See Leila Amos Pendleton, "Our New Possessions: The Danish West Indies," *Journal of Negro History* 2, 3 (July 1917): 301.

62–4 *international prices for cotton* to *"for private sale":* George C. Rogers and James Taylor, eds., *A South Carolina Chronology, 1497–1992,* 2d ed. (USC Press, 1994), 74; *Niles Register,* 7 December 1822, quoted in Alfred G. Smith, *Economic Readjustment of an Old Cotton State: South Carolina, 1820–1860* (USC Press, 1958), 8; *Charleston Courier,* 14 May 1822.

64 *"no less than 300 sail"* to *26,744 blacks:* Elizabeth Donnan, *Documents Illustrative of the History of the Slave Trade to America*

(Carnegie Institute, 1935), "Negroes Imported into South Carolina, 1783," vol. 4, 524, 525.

65 *increase of 21 percent* to *"natural increase":* The population totals are tabulated in U. B. Phillips, "The Slave Problem in the Charleston District," *Political Science Quarterly* 22 (September 1907): 416–439, reprinted in Eugene Genovese, ed., *The Slave Economy of the Old South,* 202. The "natural increase" among the slave population during these decades of a positive 2 percent, southern-wide, is well documented and explained in William Robert Fogel, *Without Consent or Contract: The Rise and Fall of American Slavery* (W.W. Norton, 1994), 123–124, 127.

The demographic implication is that, on the eve of Vesey's revolt in 1822, the Charleston District contained, although not a majority of African immigrants, a majority of black inhabitants as a result of the "natural increase" of the generation enslaved from 1800 onward, and the probable continued residence within the Charleston counties of the younger African slaves imported in the late eighteenth century, such as Denmark Vesey himself. (A comparison of the prices brought by "prime field hands" in the Charleston District with prices for similar slaves at plantations in Middle Georgia for 1800–1813 indicates that until the 1820s there was little economic benefit or market for the Charleston masters to sell off their newly acquired Africans outside their city's district. See Phillips, "Slave Problem," in Genovese, ed., *Slave Economy,* 211.)

Thus, Vesey had a potential pool of black recruits who overwhelmingly outnumbered their white masters and, within that pool of recruits, Vesey could find a significant plurality of first- and second-generation Africans and African-Americans. By the year of his attempted revolt, 1822, both the black majority and the African plurality were facing a "sell-off" as economic hard times settled upon Carolina cotton planters, and as Middle Georgia prices for slaves exceeded Charleston District prices.

"fairy spots": Robert Mills, *Statistics* (Hubert and Lloyd, 1826), 463.

65–6 *"the whites are going to create"* to *"would be right to do it": Official Report,* "Trial of Peter Poyas, Testimony of Witness No. 5," 51.

66 *"our church was shut up"* to *"we were fully able"*: Ibid., "Trial of Jesse Blackwood, Confession," 58.

66–7 *"Vesey was in the habit"* to *"I felt as if I was bound"*: Ibid., "Trial of Monday Gell, Confession," 72; "Trial of Bacchus Hammett, Confession," 110; "Examination of Billy [Bulkley]," 180; "Trial of Smart Anderson, Confession," 89–90; "Trial of Gullah Jack, Testimony of Witness No. 10," 74; "Extracts," 164–165; "Trial of Gullah Jack, Confession of Harry Haig," 79.

68 *Bulkley Farm rituals:* Ibid., "Introduction," 4.

68–9 *"to take every ship"* to *welcome at Port-au-Prince:* Ibid., "Trial of Jesse Blackwood, Confession," 59; "Trial of Monday Gell, Confession," 71; "Confession of John Enslow," 111; "Extracts," 160. The three ships departing Charleston for Santo Domingo—the *Volunt,* the *Samuel-Smith,* and the *Northumberland*—are listed in the *Charleston Courier,* "Shipping News," 7 May, 16 May, and 21 May 1822.

69 *that "they should assume":* Official Report, "Narrative," 21.

69–70 *"A Fine Green Turtle"* to *"We have lived":* Charleston Courier, 7 June 1822; 11 June 1822.

70 *"put to instant death"* to *"But take care":* Official Report, "Trial of Jesse Blackwood, Confession," 58; "Narrative," 17. The *Official Report* describes several of Vesey's conspirators as having "yellowish" complexions, but only three—Frank Ferguson, Jack Purcell, and Pharo Thompson—are explicitly identified as mulatto.

70–1 *"something serious"* to *"remain easy under the burden":* Ibid., "Narrative," 33–34.

5. THEATER OF TERROR: THE MAGNOLIA CURTAIN AND THE SABLE CURTAIN

72 *from nine o'clock onward:* James Hamilton, Jr., *Negro Plot: An Account of the Late Intended Insurrection Among a Portion of the Blacks of the City of Charleston, South Carolina,* 2d ed. (Boston, 1822), 8–10. Official Report, "Narrative," 36.

73 *into the "black hole":* Official Report, "Narrative," 33.

"order was maintained": Duke of Saxe Weimar, Bernhard, quoted in Beatrice St. Julien Ravenel, *Architects of Charleston* (USC Press, 1994), 145.

73–5 *"Beginning to fear"* to *"no confirmation of the disclosures"*: *Official Report*, "Narrative," 35; "Memorandum," 40.

76 *"domestic charade"*: William H. Freehling, *The Road to Disunion: Secessionists at Bay 1776–1854* (Oxford University Press, 1990), 61.

77–8 *"the boys had been taken up for stealing"* to *"go upstairs and kill his master and family"*: *Official Report*, "Trial of Peter Poyas, Testimony of Witness No. 5," 51; "Trial of Samuel Guifford, a free Negro, and Robert Hadden, a free mulatto, both of them boys," 59–60; "Narrative, James Ferguson's Reply," 21, 76.

79 *"To kill you"*: Quoted in correspondence, Martha Proctor Richardson to James Richardson, 7 August 1822, Southern Historical Collection, Chapel Hill, NC.

79–80 *He told Blackwood . . . fatal to him*: *Official Report*, "Trial of Jesse Blackwood, Confession," 57–58; Hamilton, *Negro Plot*, 10.

81 *"that the fact was really so"*: Hamilton, *Negro Plot*, 8; *Official Report*, "Narrative," 36; W. H. Wilson, *Reminiscences of William Hasell Wilson (1811–1902)* (Patterson and White Co., 1937), 5–6.

81–2 *four hundred of the state militia . . . had hired spies*: "Regimental Orders—17th Regiment," 1822, SCHS; Governor Thomas Bennett to Commander G. W. Cross, 17 June 1822, SCDAH; Hamilton, *Negro Plot*, 6–7, 10.

83 *"I shall never forget"* to *"in a populous town"*: Wilson, *Reminiscences*, 6–7; Hamilton, *Negro Plot*, 10.

84–5 *"there was a sort of disagreement"* to *"he would let them know"*: *Official Report*, "Narrative," 24–25; "Trial of Denmark Vesey, Evidence of William Paul," 62; "Confessions of Jesse Blackwood," 58; "Trial of Harry Haig, Testimony of Witness No. 10," 80.

86 *"enjoyed so much the confidence"* to *"everyone, even the women"*: Ibid., "Narrative," 29; "Trial of Denmark Vesey, Testimony of Witness No. 9," 65.

87 *seized Denmark Vesey*: Ibid., "Extracts No. 8," 161; Hamilton, *Negro Plot*, 18.

6. THE TRIALS OF VESEY AND HIS CONSPIRATORS

88 *"Die like a man!"*: Thomas Higginson, "Denmark Vesey," reprinted in full in *Black Rebellion: Selections from Travelers and Outlaws* (Arno Press, 1969), 230.

88–9 *Hamilton authorized this group* to *"were not repugnant to"*: James Hamilton, Jr., *Negro Plot: An Account of the Late Intended Insurrection Among a Portion of the Blacks of the City of Charleston, South Carolina*, 2d ed. (Boston, 1822), 12; *Official Report*, "Introduction," 2–3.

89 *"had not had a fair trial"*: Vesey quoted in Beach correspondence, 5 July 1822.

90–2 *"Melancholy Effect"* to *"Court, under the influence"*: *Charleston Courier*, 21 June and 29 June 1822.

92 *"the testimony of one witness"*: *Official Report*, "Introduction," 3.

93 *"would not like"* to *"was about religion"*: Ibid., "Trial of Denmark Vesey, Evidence of William Paul," 62; "Evidence of Benjamin Ford," 64.

94 *"Good God!"* to *"we'll not want men"*: Ibid., "Narrative," 27–28, 26.

"Charleston stumbled": Richard C. Wade, *Slavery in the Cities: The South 1820–1860* (Oxford University Press, 1964), 240–241.

95 *disproved in part*: Robert Starobin, "Denmark Vesey's Slave Conspiracy of 1822: A Study in Rebellion and Repression," in *American Slavery: The Question of Resistance*, ed. John Bracey (Wadsworth, 1971), 142–155; William H. Freehling, *Prelude to Civil War: The Nullification Controversy in South Carolina, 1816–1836* (Harper & Row, 1966), 52–54; William H. Freehling, "Denmark Vesey's Peculiar Reality," in *New Perspectives on Race and Slavery*, eds. Robert Abzug and Stephen Maizlish (University of KY Press, 1986), 36–39.

value of Charleston cotton: Alfred G. Smith, *Economic Readjustment of an Old Cotton State: South Carolina 1820–1860* (USC Press, 1958), "Appendix: Monthly Range of Short Staple Cotton Prices in the Charleston Market, 1815–1833," 220–223. The Charleston District also exported long-staple Sea Islands cotton, but the prices of this commodity followed the market decline of short-staple cotton in this same period before and during Vesey's revolt. Commercial credit to plantation producers of either cotton in South Carolina concentrated exclusively among locally owned banks at Charleston, exacerbating the economic depression in that city.

96 *"By a vote of the court"* to *"But this not producing"*: *Official Report,* "Introduction," 9; "Narrative," 30.

97 *Colonel George Warren Cross:* Consolidated Index of South Carolina, 1695–1925, SCDAH (32169); *Official Report,* "Trial of Denmark Vesey," 61; see also John Belton O'Neall, *Biographical Sketches of the Bench and Bar of South Carolina,* vol. 2 (S. G. Courtenay & Co., 1859), 258–259.

98 *"Denmark Vesey"* to *tears on Denmark Vesey's face: Official Report,* "Sentence on Denmark Vesey," 135; "Narrative," 30.

7. THE SHOCK OF EXECUTIONS: DENMARK VESEY AS A NATIONAL FIGURE

100 *"Ah! Slavery is":* Beach correspondence, 5 July 1822.

101 *Independent Congregational Circular Church:* George N. Edwards, *History of the Independent or Congregational Church of Charleston* (Pilgrim Press, 1947), 32–35, 46–47. Mrs. Beach was the widow of Dr. Samuel Beach, a former assistant pastor of the Circular Church. See "Samuel Beach," in *Princetonians 1776–1783: A Biographical Dictionary* (Princeton University Press, 1981), 397–400.

101–2 *"When interrogated"* to *"was particularly observed":* Beach correspondence, 5 July 1822.

102 *"not in a very supplicating tone"* to *"I suppose you'll let me": Official Report,* "Narrative," 31.

"the Negroes were under": Beach correspondence, 5 July 1822.

wraith of Denmark Vesey: Ibid., 15 July 1822.

102–3 *"I heard that Vesey"* to *"I am told":* Ibid., 5 July 1822.

103 *unspecified site at Blake's Lands* to *"At its edge":* John Bennett, *The Doctor to the Dead: Grotesque Legends and Folk Tales of Old Charleston* (USC Press, 1995), 66–67.

103–4 *"immense crowds"* to *"They generally got":* Thomas Higginson, "Denmark Vesey," reprinted in full in *Black Rebellion: Selections from Travelers and Outlaws* (Arno Press, 1969), 265.

104 *"Ashley Avenue Oak"*: "Denmark Vesey" listing in *Kaiser Index to Black Resources. 1948–1986*, ed. Schomburg Center for Research in Black Culture of the New York Public Library (Carlson Publishing, 1992), vol. 5, 269. Ashley Avenue was known as Rutledge Avenue in the nineteenth century.

105 *fired shots at the Charleston mail coach*: *Charleston Courier*, 17 July 1822; Beach correspondence, 15 July 1822.

105–6 *"All the African Church"* to *"Morris Brown knew"*: *Official Report*, "Trial of Peter Poyas, Testimony of William Paul," 53; "Confession of Monday Gell," 69.

106 *"Among the conspirators"*: James Hamilton, Jr., *Negro Plot: An Account of the Late Intended Insurrection Among a Portion of the Blacks of the City of Charleston, South Carolina*, 2d ed. (Boston, 1822), 31.

107 *an "immense crowd"*: Beach correspondence, 25 July 1822.

108 *"Owing to some bad arrangement"*: "A Colored American," *The Late Contemplated Insurrection in Charleston, S.C. . . . .* (New York: 1850; n.p.), 4–9.

"I have now passed": Quoted in Donald G. Morgan, *Justice William Johnson: The First Dissenter* (USC Press, 1954), 138.

109 *"I do not believe they would bring any price"*: John Potter to Langdon Cheves, 16 July 1822, SCHS.

"Ours as yet" to *"young man, Hamilton"*: Beach correspondence, 23 July and 25 July 1822.

109–10 *"White men, too, would engender"* to *"As yet nothing"*: These newspaper notices are quoted in Robert Starobin, "Denmark Vesey's Slave Conspiracy of 1822: A Study in Rebellion and Repression," in *American Slavery: The Question of Resistance*, ed. John Bracey (Wadsworth, 1971), 86–91, and in Higginson, "Denmark Vesey," 265–267.

110 *"As a very general desire"* to *"Although a different style"*: *Official Report*, "Introduction," 1.

112 *"she was cautiously told"*: Quoted in Higginson, "Denmark Vesey," 274–275.

"a scheme so wicked" to *"hero of Charleston"*: Hamilton, *Negro Plot*, 8; Virginia L. Glenn, "James Hamilton, Jr., of South Carolina: A Biography" (Ph.D. diss., 1964, UNC), 28.

113 *"humanity wept"* to *"The evil is entailed":* Governor Bennett's
address is quoted in D. D. Wallace, *The History of South Carolina,*
vol. 2 (American Historical Society Publishers, 1934), 417.

114 *"If such be the law":* Quoted in Donald G. Morgan, *Justice William
Johnson: The First Dissenter* (USC Press, 1954), 138.

"I have heard" to *"has almost":* Beach correspondence, 5 July 1822.

"in quelling the disturbances": U.S. Secretary of War John C. Calhoun
to Maj. James Bankhead, 22 July 1822, in *The Papers of John C.
Calhoun, 1822–1823,* vol. 2, ed. Edwin Hemphill (USC Press, 1973),
219. Joel R. Poinsett, one of the conspiracy's prosecutors and
judges, later successor to Calhoun as U.S. secretary of war, wrote
to Calhoun in July 1822, reproposing the eighteenth-century
ambition of cutting a canal across the Charleston peninsula "from
river to river." Such a canal would have permanently separated
the city from the contiguous United States, thereby, in Poinsett's
argument, providing "a better line of defense than the present
one." Calhoun was interested in the idea. Ibid.

115 *the Citadel was established:* "Citadel," in *Encyclopedia of Southern
Culture,* eds. Charles Reagan Wilson et al. (UNC Press, 1989),
277–278.

116 *"nightly communications"* to *His grave:* Glenn, "James Hamilton,
Jr., of South Carolina," 418, 420–421.

8. THE DARKNESS OF SLAVERY: DENMARK VESEY
AS A HISTORICAL FIGURE

117 *"Remember Denmark Vesey":* Frederick M. Holland, ed., Frederick
Douglass, "Men of Color to Arms!" in *Frederick Douglass: Colored
Orator* (Haskell House, 1969), 297–298.

118 *"Could the prejudices":* *Niles Register,* 27 September 1823.

President James Monroe chose to delay indefinitely action: See the message dispatched by Monroe on 25 February 1823 to the United
States Senate in response to Senate queries, after Denmark
Vesey's attempted revolt, regarding U.S. commercial trade with
the "Island of St. Domingo" and the recognition of the black revolutionary government there. Monroe acknowledged in his
response that such queries "suppose something peculiar in the

nature of that island, and in the character of its population, to which attention is due."

Monroe continues in this same message to the senators that the "establishment of a government of a people of color in the island, on the principles above stated, evinces, distinctively, the idea of a separate interest and a distrust of other nations. . . . To what extent that spirit may be indulged, or to what purposes applied, our experience is yet too limited to enable us to inform a just estimate." *Annals of the Congress of the United States, Seventeenth Congress, Second Session* (Gales and Seaton, 1855), 285.

119 *existed among the French Negroes: Official Report,* "Trial of Louis Remoussin," 83.

"The question of slavery": Hayne's speech quoted in D. D. Wallace, *The History of South Carolina,* vol. 2 (American Historical Society Publishers, 1934), 417.

"We are sorry to see": National Intelligencer, 31 August 1822.

120 *"like a firebell in the night":* Thomas Jefferson to John Holmes, 22 April 1820, in *The Works of Thomas Jefferson, Federal Edition,* vol. 12 (G. P. Putnam, 1905), 158.

121 *"a few moments"* to *"Congress has made us free": Official Report,* "Confessions of Jack Purcell," 87–88, 12.

122 *"band of patriots":* "A Colored American," *The Late Contemplated Insurrection in Charleston, S.C.* (New York, 1850), 4–9. The attribution of authorship is marked in pencil on the copy of this anonymous booklet at the Schomburg Center for Research in Black Culture of the New York Public Library.

example of black resistance: Martin R. Delany, *Blake, or The Huts of America* (Beacon Press 1970), 112–113.

123 *Alfred and Lavinia Sanders:* Larry Koger, *Black Slaveowners: Free Black Slavemasters in South Carolina, 1790–1860* (McFarland & Company, 1985), 177. Peter Prioleau was also known as Peter Desvaneys in the city after his betrayal of the Vesey conspiracy and his subsequent manumission.

123–4 *"There is no [military] reason"* to *"a willingness to look":* Thomas Higginson, "Denmark Vesey," reprinted in full in *Black Rebellion:*

Selections from Travelers and Outlaws (Arno Press, 1969), 263, 265, 268.

125 **Robert Vesey:** Frank [Frances] A. Rollins, *Life and Public Service of Martin R. Delany* (Lee and Shepard, 1883), reprinted in *Two Biographies by African-American Women* (Oxford University Press, 1991), 193–194. See also Robert Rosen, *Confederate Charleston* (USC Press, 1994), 153.

the names recorded: "State Free Negro Capitation Tax Books, Charleston, S.C., 1841–1846, 1848–ca. 52, 1855, 1857, 1860," SCDAH. The destruction or loss of these tax books, possibly informative about Vesey, was likely the result of a scornful ignorance of black history rather than a political conspiracy by the state. Nine of the tax books were saved in the early twentieth century by the scholar Dr. J. W. Babcock, who found them "amid trash thrown out of the State House" at Columbia, South Carolina. See the "Pamphlet Accompanying South Carolina Microcopy Number 11," SCDAH.

127 *short run to mixed reviews: New York Times,* 4 November 1948, 38:2.

127–8 *"like Communist conspiracies in our own day":* Stanley M. Elkins, *Slavery: A Problem in American Institutional and Intellectual Life,* 2nd ed. (University of Chicago Press, 1968), 138.

128 *"Vesey's example must":* Sterling Stuckey, "Remembering Denmark Vesey: Agitator or Insurrectionist?" *Negro Digest,* February 1966, 41.

128–9 *"the country's tensest civil rights struggle"* to *black "rebels":* Walter J. Fraser, Jr., *Charleston, Charleston!: The History of a Southern City* (UNC Press, 1989), 421–423; *New York Times,* 22 July 1969, 38:2.

129 *Secretary Robert Finch:* Ralph David Abernathy, *And the Walls Came Tumbling Down: An Autobiography* (Harper & Row, 1989), 569.

130 *"home memorabilia": Charleston News and Courier,* 25 Feb. 1951, A1, 23 Aug. 1973, B1. "Ashley Avenue Oak," in "Information for Guides of Historical Charleston," unpublished monograph, SCHS, 482.

9. REMEMBERING DENMARK VESEY AS
A BLACK LEADER

131 *"What [is] the use":* Official Report, "Confession of Smart Anderson," 90.

132 *"remain slaves"* to *"more than he feared his God":* Ibid., "Narrative," 12.

133 *"the condition of the people":* Charleston Courier, 12 May 1865.
"of the great insurrectionary": Ibid., 13 May 1865.
"We must unite": Official Report, "Confession of Rolla Bennett," 46.

134 *"would not protect him"* to *"that if we did not put":* Ibid., "Trial of Gullah Jack, Evidence of Witness No. 10," 77; "Narrative," 4; "Trial of Rolla Bennett, Evidence of Witness No. 1," 43.

134–5 *"Integration is not good"* to *"The only real solution":* Malcolm X, Malcolm X: Speeches at Harvard, ed. Archie Epps (Paragon, 1991), 126–127, 140.

136–7 *"I beg you"* to *"he was as willing as anybody":* Official Report, "Trial of Mingo Harth, Evidence of William Paul," 86; "Trial of Denmark Vesey, Evidence of William Paul," 61; "Trial of Prince Graham," 124–125.

138 *written in "Arabick":* James W. Hagy, "Some Examples of Non-European Religious and Ethnic Diversity in South Carolina Prior to 1861," SCHS Carologue, Spring 1993, 25.
"Muslim superiority": Michael A. Gomez, "Muslims in Early America," Journal of Southern History 60, no. 4 (November 1994): 700–701.
had a personal fascination: Official Report, "Narrative," 11.

139 *"Go Down Moses":* Vincent Harding, There Is a River: The Black Struggle for Freedom in America (Harcourt Brace Jovanovich, 1981), 69; Marion Starkey, Striving to Make It My Home: The Story of Americans from Africa (W. W. Norton, 1964), 179.
"if he did not do it for himself" to *"This was the fact":* Beach correspondence, 5 July 1822.

140 *divine rightness of their servitude:* Eugene Genovese, In Red and Black: Marxian Exploration in Southern and Afro-American History (Vintage Books, 1971), 145–146; Eugene Genovese, Roll, Jordan, Roll: The World the Slaves Made (Pantheon Books, 1974), 186–187.

141 *"After being treated as things"* to that *"the seminal"*: Cone quoted in
Theo Wituliet, *The Way of the Black Messiah* (Meyerstone Books,
1987), 165; James H. Cone and Gayraud S. Wilmore, "Black Theology and African Theology: Consideration for Dialogue, Cri-
tique, and Integration," in *Black Theology: A Documentary History
1966–1979*, eds. Cone et al. (Orbis Books, 1979), 468.

142 *"'Do not open'"*: G. Clarke Chapman, Jr., "Black Theology and
Theology of Hope: What Have They to Say to Each Other?" in
Black Theology, eds. Cone et al., 207.

"two souls": W. E. B. Du Bois, *The Souls of Black Folk* (Dodd, Mead,
1967), 16.

POSTSCRIPT: A PERSONAL CONCLUSION:
SPARTACUS'S LIST AND THE SEARCH
FOR VESEY'S GRAVE

144 *"a man of supreme daring"* to *"In accordance with"*: Gaius Julius
Caesar, *The Battle for Gaul*, trans. Anne Wiseman et al. (David R.
Godine, 1980), 24, 90.

146 *"If, for some reason"*: Stephen Jay Gould, "Jurassic Park," in *Past
Imperfect: History According to the Movies*, ed. Mark C. Carnes
(Henry Holt, 1995), 32.

147 *what was Blake's lands*: Samuel Gaillard Stoney, *This Is Charleston*
(Carolina Art Association, 1944), 129. See also Henry A. M.
Smith, *Rivers and Regions of Early South Carolina* (The Reprint
Company, 1988), vol. 3, 35.

148 *"the digging of the graves"*: Petition of M. P. Belknap to the South
Carolina Senate and House of Representatives, 14 December
1822, SCDAH.

Bodies of criminals executed in Charleston were sometimes
offered by the city, "if desired," to local surgeons for dissection;
but the minutes of the meetings of the Charleston Medical Society for 1822 record no such use of the remains of Vesey or his conspirators. See the archives of the Medical University of South
Carolina Library, Charleston, South Carolina.

149 *marked as "Potters Field"*: Charleston map, circa 1820, SCHS.

150 *several human bones:* Interview with Ernestine C. Fellers, archivist, city of Charleston, May 1998.

151 *"burnt on the Work-house Green":* "Magazine Street," in "Information for Guides of Historical Charleston," unpublished monograph, SCHS, 328–330.

infamous Newgate Prison: St. Julien Ravenel, *Architects,* 126. In this early-twentieth-century work, Ravenel also provided history and plates of the former Potter's Field along Ashley Avenue, 189, 192–193.

153 *"tears trickled down his cheeks":* *Official Report,* "Narrative," 30.

INDEX

Paul, William, 70, 75, 77, 81, 159
 arrest and interrogation of, 73–4, 79
 testimony of, 105, 136
Payne, William, 64
Pencil, William, 71, 77, 82
Philadelphia, 114
 colonial, 16, 17
Phillips, W. B., 174
Poinsett, Joel R., 187
Polly (ship), 26, 33
Pompey (Gnaeus Pompeius Magnus), 145
Porgy and Bess (Heyward and Gershwin), 126, 127, 152
Port Royal, Battle of, 7
Potter, John, 109
Potter's Field (Charleston), 149–50
Poyas, Peter, 55, 56, 58, 61, 65, 67, 80, 84, 92, 97, 111, 136, 146, 159
 arrest of, 85, 86, 163
 assignment during insurrection of, 60
 commands of silence to followers of, 142
 execution of, 101, 103, 160
 Hamilton's suspicions of, 82
 house servants mistrusted by, 70
 interrogation of, 74–5, 77
 list of potential recruits kept by, 59
 missionary visits to jail cell of, 101–2
 Paul's denunciation of, 73

Presbyterians, 8, 35, 106, 177
Prioleau, Col. John C., 70, 72–3
Prioleau, Peter, 70–2, 77, 81, 82, 123, 124, 188
Pritchard, Jack (Gullah Jack), 48, 53, 56, 58, 78, 84, 85, 111, 157–9
 arrest of, 105
 assignment during insurrection of, 60
 execution of, 106, 160–1
 and police raid on A.M.E. church, 51
 as shaman, 48–9, 67–8, 102, 133, 161
 weapons hidden by, 61, 66, 93, 162
Purcell, Jack, 121, 133, 161, 182

Quincy, Josiah, 19

Ramsey, David, 163
Ravenel, St. Julien, 181
Reconstruction, 82
"Remembering Denmark Vesey: Agitator or Insurrectionist?" (Stuckey), 128
Remoussin, Louis, 119
Robert Mills Manor (Charleston), 151–2
Robertson, Adam, 161
Robertson, John, 161–2
Robertson, Robert, 162
Roman Catholic Church, 10, 141